"Here one finds a robust, honest, and thorough guide for all who are facing important decisions at this moment in Methodist history. The authors have firsthand and intimate knowledge of the theological divide in The United Methodist Church, and they bring considerable experience to the task of answering our questions. We owe them our gratitude for this indispensable resource for churches and pastors."

—*Bill T. Arnold, PhD*
Paul S. Amos Professor of Old Testament Interpretation
School of Biblical Interpretation, Asbury Theological Seminary

"There is a great restlessness within our tribe. Every day, I hear from pastors and church leaders who are frustrated, discouraged, and starving for level-headed guidance as they navigate the complicated and politically charged path out of the United Methodist Church. But these leaders are not just looking for a way out. They are hungrily searching for a vision that will re-energize weary congregations and breathe new life into the Methodist way. This book offers that kind of hope. It is a handbook of practical tools for launching vision-level conversations, and a clarion call for a more vibrant, faithful, Spirit-led Methodism than we have known. I could not be more excited about what is ahead. I urge you to join us in building a movement whose time has come."

—*Dr. Carolyn Moore*
Chair of the Global Council of the Wesleyan Covenant Association
Lead Pastor, Mosaic Church - Evans, Georgia

"In the midst of decision-making, local United Methodist Congregations find themselves with multiple questions and difficulty locating trusted sources to find answers. This volume of work provides answers to those questions by trusted leaders. The comprehensive information found in this text offers churches an understanding of why they should consider leaving the United Methodist Church, while also providing details of the polity and structure of the Global Methodist Church. This is a must-have resource for churches in the discernment process."

—*Dr. Leah Hidde-Gregory*
Global Methodist Church Organizer
Mid-Texas Transitional Conference Academy

"When so much is uncertain, it is reassuring to have this illuminating word from two respected, tested, and hopeful leaders. Multiplying Methodism is required reading for Methodist congregations and church members seeking to discern a faithful future."

"Since the adjournment of the 2019 session of General Conference, I have joined other voices, both progressive and conservative, in acknowledging the need for a "multiplication" of The Methodist Movement. The theological, missional, and covenantal differences within The United Methodist Church have caused harm to one another, those we attempt to serve, and our shared witness for too long. Today, faithful United Methodists are actively discerning God's call upon their individual lives and the life of their congregation. That discernment will lead some to continue to serve and live within The United Methodist Church and others to move into a new expression of the Wesleyan Way. I'm grateful that my friends, Dr. Jeff Greenway, and Bishop Mike Lowry have provided a resource to be used for those considering becoming a part of The Global Methodist Church. This resource should not be viewed in a forbidding way, but rather as a tool for clarity and prayerful decision-making; allowing us to help one another move and live fully into the ministry and mission God is calling toward and we hope for. I know this book will be an important contribution to the work of prayer and discernment many are engaged in. May the Spirit of Christ be the guide."

MULTIPLYING METHODISM

A bold witness of Wesleyan faith at the dawn
of the Global Methodist Church

Jeff Greenway
and Mike Lowry

ISBN (paperback): 978-1-7379112-5-8
ISBN (ebook): 978-1-7379112-6-5

313 Publishing
Columbus, Ohio

Printed in the United States of America.

Cover and Interior Design: Bogdan Matei
Editor: Vicki L. Rich

CONTENTS

ACKNOWLEDGMENTS

One day, a pastor was walking in a park and was approached by a father carrying his daughter on his shoulders. The pastor greeted them, looked the little girls in the eye, and said, "My aren't you big!" The little girl giggled, looked both ways as if she was looking to see if anyone else was watching, leaned forward as if sharing a secret, and said, "This isn't all me!"

The same can be said of us. We came to this faith very differently. Bishop Lowry came from a place of liberal skepticism but has been converted to the faith "once for all entrusted to the saints." Jeff Greenway was born into the family of an evangelical, United Methodist pastor and his wife, and has never known a time he didn't believe Jesus is who He said He is and did everything He promised He would do. As we were writing this book, we were keenly aware we stand on the shoulders of others who have come before us, walk beside us, and encourage us along the way.

First, we thank God for our wives, Jolynn Lowry and Beth Greenway. The value of their selfless sacrifice enabling each of us to pursue God's call on our lives can never be calculated. We are both better because we've shared our lives with them.

We thank God for our families. Those who have gone before us have left their fingerprints all over us, and our children and grandchildren are our greatest legacy of faith and love. They have also sacrificed in ways most people cannot comprehend, and we are profoundly thankful for their love and support.

We thank God for those who've taught and discipled us. From Sunday school teachers to seminary professors—from small group leaders to covenant group members—from noted authors to salt of the earth saints in every church we've served—from thought leaders to humble servants—from bishops and superintendents to colleagues who freely shared their wisdom—each of these groups of people and more have helped to shape us into the followers of Jesus we are today.

We offer a special word of gratitude for those churches we have been blessed to pastor: Rich Square Friends in Indiana, St. Paul's UMC in Kerrville, Texas, Wesley UMC in Harlingen, Texas, Asbury UMC in Corpus Christi, Texas, Bethany UMC in Austin, Texas and University UMC in San Antonio by Bishop Lowry; First UMC in Butler, PA, Christ UMC in Erie and the Reynoldsburg UMC in Reynoldsburg, OH by Dr. Jeff Greenway. Each of these faith communities has shaped and formed us as much as we shaped and formed them.

We thank God for those who have helped to take this book from thought to reality. Andy Miller from Seedbed gave us some very good strategic feedback, and Vicki Rich from 313 Publishing has turned our rough manuscript into a finished product.

It's our prayer that anything contained in these pages that is not centered in the truth of Jesus will do no harm and fall to the ground as if never written or spoken, but if anything contained in these pages is centered in the truth of Jesus, may it stir such a response in the reader that action ensues.

Grace and peace,
Jeff Greenway and Mike Lowry
July 28, 2022

INTRODUCTION:
START WITH WHY

As we begin, we acknowledge that some of our readers are experiencing various stages of awareness and grief about what's happening in the United Methodist Church. To be honest—we're not quite sure how to process it. The United Methodist Church has been moving toward a proposed amicable separation for the last several years. The 2019 endorsement of the Protocol of Grace and Reconciliation through Separation by a broad range of United Methodist leaders and diverse caucus groups appeared to ease tensions and pointed toward a peaceful resolution of our decades-long denominational conflict. But two years, a global pandemic, and three General Conference postponements later—the dream of the Protocol or any form of amicable separation seems like a distant memory.

Those charged with guarding and protecting the institution appear to have successfully stopped the Protocol and are increasingly making it difficult for people who desperately want to separate from each other to do so. While we're disappointed, we're not surprised. It's to be expected. The Empire always strikes back.

I (Jeff Greenway) remember something my friend and iterative thinker Chris Ritter said several years ago. He said, "It is likely the new Methodism we yearn for will be born in battle." We have hoped the negotiated agreements would hold, but they have not, and it appears Chris was right. It doesn't appear the United Methodist Church and those charged with preserving it are going to allow those who yearn to live into what has been prayed for and planned for the last several years without it costing something. Our prayer is it doesn't cost us our souls.

Let us say a word to those readers who may be institutional representatives committed to protecting what was. The issues that divide us didn't magically disappear during the pandemic. Nor will they disappear with a change of a few lines in *The Book of Discipline*.

We humbly request we work together in any way we can to capture the spirit of the Protocol and find creative and healthy ways we can bless and send our respective understandings of the faithful witness of Methodism into the future—rather than return to old and tired ways of continuing to fight and tear apart the church. The world outside our church buildings and General Conference—which includes many who are in desperate need of Jesus—won't be helped if this matter spills out into the headlines and ends up in civil court.

So, here we are, a couple of pastors who've given our adult and professional lives serving the United Methodist Church in a wide variety of ways. Together we have over 73 years of experience as ordained clergy in the United Methodist Church. We have both pastored local congregations for decades. One of us (Jeff Greenway) has served as a District Superintendent and Seminary president. The other (Bishop Mike Lowry) has recently finished serving thirteen-and-a-half years as the resident bishop of the Central Texas Conference and served on the Executive Committee of the Council of Bishops during the 2012 – 2016 quadrennium. We've been delegates to multiple General Conferences and rendered service on various denominational boards. Active engagement as leaders in the conferences we've served in has been an ongoing part of our lives. We love the church and are deeply invested in it. And yet, we write discussing why we should separate from our present denomination and help form the Global Methodist Church. The weight and history of this moment are not lost on us.

We're reminded of a powerful scene from *The Lord of the Rings* by J.R.R. Tolkien. Early in the story, the good wizard, Gandalf, explains the history of the Ring to the young hobbit, Frodo Baggins. This mystical ring has been lost to the world of men for centuries until it's found by Gollum—a strange creature whose entire appearance was transformed by the ugliness that comes with trying to hold onto power (which the Ring symbolizes). The rediscovery of the Ring also corresponds with the rise of the dark wizard, Sauron—and the advance of evil on Middle Earth. As he comes to grips with the weight of this moment in time, Frodo—the most unlikely of heroes—laments: "I wish it need not have happened in my time."

Frodo knows something he can't *not* know and feels the weight of responsibility to do something. The good wizard Gandalf speaks a word of wisdom in response to Frodo and to us: "So do I, and so do all who live to see such times. But that is not for them to decide. All we have to decide is what to do with the time that is given us."[1]

We can relate. We wish this season in the life of the United Methodist Church hadn't happened in our time, but here we are. We have decided what to do with the time that's been given to us. The words of Mordecai to Esther reverberate in our hearts and minds. "For if you keep silent at this time, relief and deliverance will rise for the Jews from another place, but you and your father's family will perish. Who knows? Perhaps you have come to royal dignity for just such a time as this."[2] We have come to believe that God is calling us to spend a portion of that time here at the dawn of the New Methodism to write a case for why we believe it's time to leave the United Methodist Church and join the newly formed Global Methodist Church.

As we write, we understand people are resistant to change. The pattern is so dependable that Newton's First Law of Motion describes it: "Everything continues in a state of rest unless it is compelled to change by forces impressed upon it."

We resist change and often only embrace it when we're compelled to do so. Over the years, we've sometimes led change well, and other times—not so well. About eight years ago, I (Jeff Greenway) learned an important lesson about leading change while reading a best-selling book by Simon Sinek.[3]

You have to start with why. When leading change well, one has to begin by explaining why the change is necessary. Why the shift is important. Why the change is crucial to the mission. We need to start with why because people who resist change may embrace it if we can make the case for why it's necessary. If we want to lead change well in our homes, at our schools, in our workplaces, in our communities, and especially in the church, we start by answering why it's necessary.

Let us try to explain how this works by first explaining when it doesn't. When most of us want something to change, we usually identify what it is. The first question many folks try to answer when leading change is the "what?" question. The answer to this question is often based on logic and reason.

"What?" Is the head question—and its answers are designed to reach a logical solution or goal. However, the head isn't the seat of the deepest decision-making of our lives, and when only the head is involved, it becomes easy for those who do not like "what" we're describing to rationalize against the change. We get bogged down in resistance to "what" the change is, and we never get to the "why."

The next question most folks address when attempting to lead change is "how?" They describe strategies and techniques that will be used to explain how they plan to accomplish the "what."

"How?" Is the heart question—and it appeals to the feeling level. Sometimes we are willing to change because we believe it will make us feel better, but most change is messy and it's almost impossible to always feel good about it. While it's closer to our place of deepest decision-making, when the heart is involved, it's easy for those who don't like "what" we're describing and "how" we propose doing it to rally militant antagonism against the change—and we never get to the "why." It's not hard to see this at play in the present atmosphere of the United Methodist Church.

The last question most folks address is "why?" This is the question most three-year-olds ask first, do you know "why?" It is the question of the will. A three-year-old doesn't have highly defined reasoning abilities when making decisions—so "what" isn't always important. A three-year-old has feelings, but they can change quickly and are not the basis for most of their decisions—so "how" isn't always important. However, a three-year-old has a strong will, and they constantly want to know "why" before they want to know "how" and "what."

"Why" goes further than the tactics and logic of the head, and deeper than the feelings of the heart. The will is the deepest place of our decision-making. Once the will is yielded, the heart and head soon follow. However, if the will isn't engaged and convinced, the heart and mind will never follow—resulting in unmovable opposition. The idea—the dream—the change—is dead in the water before it even starts unless the will is yielded.

Fifteen years ago, I (Jeff Greenway) was asked to chair a feasibility committee to explore building a $20 million YMCA in our community. The formation of the committee was announced in the local paper with this headline: "Committee to Study Building $20 million YMCA. The city started with "what" before we even met, and we got immediate push back because of the price tag. We described "what" was being proposed, but not "how" and "why," and folks immediately rationalized against the proposal. Their minds were closed.

We then tried to explain "how" this could be accomplished. The city was proposing an employment tax on folk who work in Reynoldsburg. It wouldn't have affected retirees and those who don't work here. It didn't matter because that was never heard. The response to "how" was open antagonism with "No New Taxes" signs appearing everywhere. Their hearts were closed.

We then tried to explain "why" by stating the new YMCA would increase property values and give our community a resource that would make our community the kind of place people want to move to, but our community had no will for the project because we started with "what" instead of "why." The proposal was dead in the water because of militant opposition before it even started.

We learned an important lesson: Don't start with "what".

In the Gospel of Luke chapter 19, we read a story about how two different groups respond to something Jesus did. Jesus was passing through Jericho on his way to Jerusalem for the last week of his life. A tax collector named Zacchaeus lived there. He had built his wealth by extorting others and was hated by everyone. As Jesus arrived, Zacchaeus (who the text says is a short guy) wanted to get a glimpse. He was an easy target in the crowd, and they didn't let him get to the front of the line to see Jesus. I envision elbows flying as folks moved to block his view. Frustrated, Zacchaeus climbed up into a tree to see Jesus as he passed by.

Then Jesus did the unexpected—he stopped, looked up, and invited himself to dinner. "All the people saw this and began to mutter, 'He has gone to be the guest of a sinner.'"[4] They could not get their heads past what Jesus was doing, and they opposed him. Of course, Jesus wasn't trying to convince them to change. He was trying to convince Zacchaeus to change, and the way Jesus engaged Zacchaeus makes all the difference in the world.

It is a reminder there is a different way to ask the same questions—that can help make the case for change. The first question to ask is "Why?" This is the question of the will—and once a person's will is engaged and yielded—people can move forward—because it solidifies the mission and minimizes opposition. Veterans of the United States Marine Corp will tell you this is the secret of their training—the surrendering of will and rebuilding it around a different priority. It takes will to run into a fight. It takes will to sacrifice for others. It takes extraordinary will to lay down one's life for a friend.[5]

Convincing someone to yield their will isn't easy. This is the hardest step, but once we answer the "why" question, and their will is yielded for the cause of the mission, the other questions become easier.

Four years ago, my city did a much better job making the case for "why" for the Recreation Center than we did fifteen years ago. It was on the spring ballot and was passed by 86% of the residents.

As Jesus made his way through the crowd, everyone wanted to get close to him. Then Jesus did the unexpected. He broke social norms and invited himself to dinner with the most unpopular guy in town. No one in Jericho that day thought Jesus had come to town for Zacchaeus! As the crowd grumbles, Jesus shows us "why." He was on a mission to help this man who was far away from God find his way back into a relationship with God. Jesus valued him. Jesus loved him. Jesus engaged him. Jesus ate with him. Something happened inside of him that evening.

The Gospel of Luke tells us "Zacchaeus stood up and said to Jesus, 'Look, Lord! Here and now I give half of my possessions to the poor, and if I have cheated anybody out of anything, I will pay back four times the amount.'"[6] Zacchaeus repented and changed his life. And at that point, Jesus revealed "why" he invited himself to Zacchaeus's house for dinner. "Jesus said to him, 'Today, salvation has come to this house, because this man, too, is a son of Abraham. For the Son of Man came to seek and to save the LOST.'"[7]

Why did Jesus eat with Zacchaeus? Because he was lost, and lost people matter to Jesus. This is a good lesson for us. Jesus started with "why." We should always start with "why"—especially when it comes to Kingdom things.

Friends, that's why we wrote this book—to share "why" we believe the time is right for traditional, orthodox Methodist Jesus-followers to leave the United Methodist Church and join the newly formed Global Methodist Church. We offer a renewed vision of the Wesleyan Movement of faith to re-embrace our shared mission of reaching those who live far away from God with the Good News of God's redeeming love in Jesus. We believe God in Christ through the power and presence of the Holy Spirit is calling us to reclaim the heart of the gospel in allegiance to Jesus as Lord and renew the Wesleyan movement throughout the world with an unapologetic embrace of the historic Christian faith.

Quite famously John Wesley, the founder of the "Methodist" or "Wesleyan" way of following Jesus as Lord, once said, *"I am not afraid that the people called Methodists should ever cease to exist either in Europe or America. But I am afraid, lest they should only exist as a dead sect, having the form of religion without the power. And this undoubtedly will be the case, unless they hold fast both the doctrine, spirit, and discipline with which they first set out."*[8]

We believe the time has come for us to once again appropriate the doctrine, spirit, and discipline which was and is at the heart of Methodism. We've written this book to help pastors and laypersons understand the issues facing the United Methodist Church and provide a rationale for separation and joining the Global Methodist Church. Section I focuses steadfastly on the "why." Why leave the United Methodist Church to join the Global Methodist

Church? Section II turns to focus on "what" a renewed vision of the Wesleyan Movement of Faith looks like in the Global Methodist Church, and "how" we envision the future of that movement.

Those who have read or listened to either of us write or speak on this subject will encounter material we have introduced and employed in other settings. We have sought to offer our shared ministry in a revised and expanded form. We hope this revised collection can serve as a source to help congregations migrate to a compelling and hopeful future in the Global Methodist Church.

We hope you enjoy the read as we start with "why." Together we have been called "for just such a time as this."[9]

SECTION I

WHY LEAVE THE UNITED METHODIST CHURCH TO JOIN THE GLOBAL METHODIST CHURCH

CHAPTER 1:
THE PRESENTING SYMPTOM

"Flee from sexual immorality. Every other sin a person
commits is outside the body, but the sexually immoral
person sins against his own body. Or do you not know that
your body is a temple of the Holy Spirit within you, whom
you have from God? You are not your own, for you were
bought with a price. So glorify God in your body."
1 Corinthians 6:18-20 (ESV)

A good physician does not jump to conclusions when a patient presents general symptoms of malaise or illness. The wise physician will spend time in conversation with the patient and asks diagnostic questions related to the presenting symptoms before running further tests to determine a clear diagnosis and course of treatment. Much of our lives would be well-served if we followed the same pattern, and instead of reacting to presenting symptoms, we took the time to make a thorough diagnosis and treatment plan.

While some have and will continue to attempt to blame the schism of the United Methodist Church and the formation of the Global Methodist Church on our decades-long internal struggle over human sexuality, we contend this is merely the presenting symptom. What's led us to the place of schism is that the presenting symptom has exposed deep and significant theological differences about foundational doctrines like the nature, role, and authority of scripture—the nature, role, and authority of Jesus—the nature of and remedy for human sin—the meaning of justification/salvation—and the meaning of Christian sanctification. We believe these differences have brought us to the place of needed separation.

We'll explore these theological differences in detail in a later chapter, but we would be negligent if we didn't address the presenting symptom at the beginning. While The United Methodist Church has official statements on human sexuality, there is great disagreement on what the Bible says about human sexuality and sexual ethics. Some hold to a traditional view rooted in the Biblical narrative that's affirmed by the overwhelming majority of the Christian world. This group understands "God's best" for human sexuality is when it is limited to a relationship between a man and a woman who live in a covenant relationship (marriage) for life. We acknowledge our sinful brokenness has led to many other forms of sexual expression but refuse to embrace them as God's best.

Others have embraced a different understanding which affirms a wide variety of sexual expressions as a good gift of God, and that demands the church affirm and celebrate a variety of sexual expressions—including but not limited to cohabitation, fornication, lesbian, gay, bisexual, transgendered, queer, and multiple partner relationships. These two views of human sexual expression have pulled the church in every different direction in large part because of the previously mentioned foundational issues, and it would be a disservice to simply blame our present impasse solely on human sexuality.

We write to share our thoughts about what the Bible says about human sexuality in the Christian tradition. We're aware this topic is emotionally charged and often causes much confusion among people of faith.

This topic is emotionally charged because our sexual identity is deeply connected to our created nature and our relationship with God. Our sexuality is the one place where we can partner with another person and God to do what only God can do—create a life. It's the very essence of our identity. When this area of our lives is used in a manner that is less-than-God's-best, it results in brokenness in the deepest part of our souls. It's our experience that this brokenness is hard to talk about—and easy to react to.

It's confusing because of the competing messages related to human sexuality in our culture. Ever since Bill Clinton had an improper relationship with Monica Lewinsky, and then parsed his words on national television when he said, "I did not have sex with that woman…"—there's been growing confusion about what "sex" is and what the ethical boundaries of sexual expression are in our culture. Watching three hours of primetime TV will expose us to every possible relational configuration and sexual circumstance seen as normal and mainstream—leading to confusion.

This is especially the case when the church is confused about its message. While the United Methodist Church has been debating human sexuality for the last 50 years, it isn't alone in being confused about its message. A 2014 article in Charisma Magazine states that statistical surveys show that the sexual behavior of "Christian" teens and young adults is statistically no different than those who don't express faith. We say we believe in Jesus, but when it comes to the practice of the gift of our sexuality, we act just like everyone else. The article called this practice "sexual atheism."[10] A quick Google search reveals countless articles with statistical support that states those who call themselves "Christian" reflect a similar sexual ethic as the larger culture.

There's a lot of confusion in this area of our lives because we live in a day of competing values about human sexuality. There are probably a wide variety of opinions about the presenting symptom among the readers of this book. We believe those who are forming the Global Methodist Church desperately need to reclaim and teach a healthy, balanced understanding of God's best when it comes to human sexuality. This will take clarity of message and the discipline to call each other to something more than reflecting the culture around us.

We don't have a sex problem—we have a sin problem. We've been created with free will. We're not just puppets. God loves us so much that he gave us the choice to love God back. However, as human beings, we struggle with our freedom. We don't always choose "God's best." We have an innate tendency to be drawn to things that are less-than-God's-best. This is called sin. It means to "stray from the path" in Hebrew, or "to miss the mark" in Greek.

It means to choose something less-than-God's-best, and by that standard—we all sin.

Not every choice we make is wrong, but we all make wrong choices. Sin is more than just an act, it's a condition of the heart that infects the human family. All of us are born with the infection of sin in our lives. Charles Wesley called this a "bent toward sinning" in his classic hymn, "Love Divine, All Loves Excelling." The question isn't: "Are we sinful?" The question for the follower of Jesus is: "Are we willing to bring our behavior under the leadership or Lordship of Jesus?" So much of our lives are determined by this choice.

In a world of competing messages about human sexuality, we need to know what God's best is when it comes to the use and exercise of this good gift from God.

So, what does the Bible say about sex? Don't worry. We're not going to be using any pictures. When trying to answer this question or any other diffi cult question of life and faith we fi nd it helpful to look at the presenting symptom through three lenses:

The Biblical/Theological Lens

We try to look through this lens without emotional attachment. What does the Bible say about human sexuality? It says plenty from beginning to end—good and bad—but God's best is rooted in the creation story and consistently messaged throughout the whole of Scripture: Sex is a good gift of God, and its created intent is between a man and a woman in marriage for life.

In the creation story, we're told, "God created humankind in his image, in the image of God he created them; male and female he created them."[11] Notice it does not say: male and two females, female and two males, male and male, or female and female, but rather male and female. Our sexuality is rooted in our created na-ture, and our call to monogamy in marriage is also rooted in the creation account. Sometimes, folks say Jesus never spoke about this, but these same words affi rming the created order were spoken by Jesus in Matthew 19:4 and Mark 10:6.

In Genesis 2:18-24, we're reminded of the intentionality and forethought with which we were created. I (Jeff Greenway) love to remind couples to remember God did not take the portion from which he fashioned the woman from the man's foot so she can be trampled over by him—or from his head so she can be dominant over him. But rather, God chose something from man's side so she could walk beside the man—from under her husband's arm so she would be protected by him—and from next to his heart so she would be cherished by him. In the end, we're told, "That is why a man leaves his father and mother and is united to his wife, and the two become one flesh."[12] We were created for mutuality and with reproductive parts that fit together.

Genesis chapters 1 and 2 reveal God's best—his created intent. It's important to remember these chapters come before Genesis 3, which records the fall of humanity into sin. The Bible also addresses all kinds of variants from God's best that human beings choose in human sexual behavior after Genesis 3. A reading of scripture will reveal examples and the implications of choosing less-than-God's-best—polygamy, adultery, bestiality, homosexuality, fornication, incest, prostitution, and other expressions of sex outside of God's created design.

This ethic which is knit into the fabric of creation has been the key to the rise of great civilizations. In 1934, J.D. Unwin, a non-Christian sociologist, studied 86 different societies over 4,000 years while attempting to determine the source of their strength and greatness. In his study, Sex and Culture, all 86 societies, non-Christian and Christian, demonstrated a direct tie between absolute heterosexual monogamy and the "expansive energy" of that civilization.[13] When the dominant practice was monogamy and fidelity in heterosexual marriage, the civilizations flourished likely because of the strong family unit. We believe this reflects God's intent for creation which is good. However, when this no longer was the dominant practice all 86 civilizations began to crumble and deteriorate—likely because of the weakness of the family unit. We believe this is a residual effect of Genesis 3.

We can say anything we want about our present cultural practices, but from the very beginning, the Bible tells us God's best, when it comes to the good gift of our human sexuality, is monogamy and fidelity (exclusive faithfulness) in the marriage of a man and a woman and celibacy (abstinence from sex) in singleness.

The Pastoral Lens

We can't help but look through this lens with emotional attachment because we're pastors and live in relationships with a wide variety of people. We do all in our power to love God and love people, but also need to be careful our expression of love is more than dysfunctional politeness. The people we serve won't be well-served if our love is mere sentiment and fails to speak and share God's truth wrapped in God's love.

When I (Jeff Greenway) think about the churches I've served, I've experienced everything from chips to nuts when it comes to sexual behavior when the congregations gathered for worship every weekend:

- The teenagers for whom oral sex is a rite of passage (the fastest growing venereal disease among teens is in the mouth).

- The adolescents who are being confused by the rising belief and increasingly common instruction that being "non-binary" is normative and acceptable.

- The high school girl giving herself away looking for approval and acceptance as she sleeps her way through various social circles.

- The college kid making his way through school as a door-to-door, unpaid gynecologist.

- The single woman who's looking for a "hook up" to try to cure her deep loneliness.

- The "friends with benefits" who change partners like shoes and often share intimacy without any emotional attachment.

- The exotic dancer who lives in shame and wants something more than what she's settled for.

- The gay man who's looking for companionship through serial partners.

- Another gay man who's chosen to live a celibate life as an act of obedience to the God who's saved him.

- The couples who are living together to see if they're compatible—even though statistics say this move before marriage dramatically reduces the chance of the relationship lasting a lifetime.

- The couples who faithfully make and keep the vows of their marriage covenant for better or worse, for richer or poorer, in sickness and in health, to love and cherish until they are parted by death.

- The six men—that I know of at the time of this writing—having affairs on their wives.

- The three women—that I know of at the time of this writing—cheating on their husbands.

- The registered sex offender who's paid a price for his crime, and lives each day as a social outcast.

- The gay couple and their kids who are trying to figure out life as they experience being loved by a Christian community.

- The 67% of "Christian" men who attend church regularly but have viewed pornography in the last month.

- The 32% of "Christian" women who attend church regularly but have unhealthy and inappropriate emotional attachments to a partner other than their husband.

I've experienced almost every possible expression of human sexual behavior in the churches I've served. Guess what? God loves them all—and so do I. Bishop Lowry can share similar stories from his 30 years as a church pastor. Together we adamantly believe God loves them all and so do both of us!

If we've just described you, there's no other place we would rather you be than engaged in a church where you're being introduced to Jesus and allowing the Holy Spirit to bring transformation into your life. Everyone is welcome in the churches we've served—everyone. But it would be less-than-loving for us not to share what we understand to be God's best for our lives.

If you are having an emotional response to what we've written or are confused about what you've heard in the past, we have the same prayer for you that the Apostle Paul had for the Jesus-followers in Ephesus who were also bombarded by a culture that had settled for far less-than-God's-best as the norm. Paul prayed: "I pray that out of his glorious riches he may strengthen you with power through his Spirit in your inner being, so that Christ may dwell in your hearts through faith. And I pray that you, being rooted and established in love, may have power, together with all the Lord's holy people, to grasp how wide and long and high and deep is the love of Christ, and to know this love that surpasses—that you may be filled to the measure of all the fullness of God."[14] The life that embodies God's best doesn't set salvation as its goal, but rather Christlikeness or sanctification. We want God's best for you.

Sometimes folks will ask us, "What about membership? Are people who choose to live a life that's less-than-God's-best allowed to become members of your church?" Well, how does God look at anything that's less-than-God's-best? God calls it sin. Have you ever chosen or settled for less-than-God's-best in your life? Have you ever deliberately sinned? Of course, you have. Same here. All of us stand on level ground at the foot of the cross, and sexual sin is just as "bad" in God's eyes as gossip, not tithing, selfishness, cheating on one's taxes, or arrogance.

It's dangerous to compare our sins with others. To think: "At least I'm not like 'them.'" Acting as if some sins are better or worse than others, and our sin, our choice of less-than-God's-best, is somehow better than someone else's more "obvious" sin is spiritual arrogance. God doesn't grade sin and the brokenness it causes on a curve. This kind of thinking gives us a false sense of superiority, but when we compare ourselves to the only One that has never sinned (Jesus) we find we can never measure up on our own and are dependent on the grace of God to save us. James tells us, "For whoever keeps the whole law and yet stumbles at just one point is guilty of breaking all of it."[15]

So, are sinners allowed to be members of God's church? We hope so. Otherwise, we should all withdraw our membership. All who are willing to profess Jesus—even though they're not perfect—are welcome in membership at the churches we serve. However, not everyone will be allowed to serve in leadership—especially if they're not willing to bring their lives under the leadership of Jesus and stop settling for less-than-God's-best.

Why? Scripture holds those who teach and lead God's church to a higher standard than others. James said it this way: "Not many of you should become teachers…because you know that we who teach will be judged more strictly."[16] This is one of the areas of our lives that we need to have under the leadership of Jesus if we're going to provide leadership to others. Therefore, for example, we wouldn't allow a person who's having an affair to serve on our Church Board, provide leadership of a Sunday school class, or be approved as a candidate for ministry.

We also won't ritualize something that isn't "God's best." Our country has given various configurations of couples the right to be united in civil unions, which some call marriage. It's a civil right. Christian marriage isn't a civil right, but it is a rite of worship of the church and will only be used in the Global Methodist Church to bless what's God's best. However, persons who aren't living God's best are welcome to worship with us in our churches, receive the sacraments, become members of our community, grow in faith, and serve in our ministries. After all, God doesn't see this sin any differently than more "white collar" sins like gossip, not tithing, or telling a lie.

The Secular Lens

We use this lens with great caution because we live in a sound-bite world that's looking for a "gotcha" quote to make those who hold a historic view of Christian marriage seem as if they are ham-fisted Luddites. While we're not perfect, our heart is to try to love people the way Jesus did, to name sin and announce grace, to show and share God's best, and announce the grace available to anyone who brings their sin and brokenness to Jesus.

If the secular press were to interview us or listen to us have this conversation with the congregations we've served, they'd likely conclude we're mean-spirited and hate people for telling them they're not living God's best. We don't hate people who settle for less-than-God's-best. Nothing could be further from the truth.

Just because we don't say "yes" to everything doesn't mean we don't love people. We constantly tell the people we serve that we love them, but more importantly God loves them and constantly calls each of us to choose his best for our lives. It's our hope this message is convicting and comforting. All are welcome. The Church is of God, and we'll provide the means of grace through which all persons can come to experience God's love and transformation in their lives. We trust God is big enough and his love is strong enough to work in human lives as we look at this emotionally charged and often confusing topic through these lenses.

In a world of competing messages about God's good gift of sexuality, we want you to know what God's best is when it comes to the use and exercise of this gift. While we know many folks in our churches may not be living God's best in this area of their lives, we're responsible for lovingly sharing God's best while reminding everyone we serve that God loves and cares for them.

I (Jeff Greenway) recently had a conversation explaining these three lenses to a couple who had settled for less-than-God's-best for this area of their lives. After finishing talking about the three lenses, I asked them, "Do you believe I love you?" They both began to cry and said, "We know you love us." I do. Even when we don't agree.

This is vitally important because this redemptive message is often lost or unspoken in many churches today with devastating results. We live in a day when the sexual boundaries of our created order have been overshadowed by a culture that values pleasure and personal freedom more than God's best as revealed in Creation and redeemed by Jesus. The result is brokenness. Sometimes the brokenness is caused by our own choices—the things we do. Other times, our brokenness is caused by the choices of others—what has been done to us. Regardless, the brokenness is real.

The New Testament letter to the Hebrews captures the essence of the Bible's teaching on sexual morality: "Marriage should be honored by all, and the marriage bed kept pure, for God will judge the adulterer and all the sexually immoral."[17] God's best intent for our sexual expression is in the context of marriage and whenever we settle for less-than-God's best, or when God's created intent is violated within us, the result is brokenness. Our sexual brokenness can shape and shade every area of our lives. Broken relationships. Broken love. Broken promises. Broken intimacy. Broken covenants. Broken trust. Brokenness.

For us to begin to live into God's best, we need to stop believing the lie Satan often whispers to us. We were created for goodness and intimacy with God and one other person. Anything else is a lie. Our created image has often been scarred by the decisions we've made or the things others have done to us but Jesus came to redeem and restore our created nature. The Apostle Paul states the possibilities this way," If anyone of us is in Christ, there is a new creation. The old things pass away and new things come."[18] Jesus saves. Jesus forgives. Jesus heals. Jesus restores. But this will not happen unless or until we lovingly and compassionately address the presenting issue in clear and redemptive ways. Our human sexuality must be brought under the command, the lordship, of Jesus Christ.

This message runs counter to today's understanding of sexuality. The pastor and congregation that speak about God's design and the best for human sexuality are often shouted down in the culture. I (Jeff Greenway) have a pastor friend who has shifted his position on human sexuality. He told me it's impossible for people to live pure lives outside of marriage and maintain fidelity within them. He says we're losing an entire generation because the church is seen as backward, narrow, and irrelevant. He contends that if the church doesn't join in being more permissive (what culture has dubbed inclusive) on human sexuality, we run the risk of being on the wrong side of history.[19]

Friends, we're not as concerned about being on the wrong side of history as we are about being on the wrong side of the Lord of History. Sexual brokenness is real, and the best, most healing answer to not to accommodate the culture, but rather lovingly and graciously lift God's best. Anything less than God's best is a lie.

CHAPTER 2:
CONTENDING FOR
THE FAITH

"Beloved, while eagerly preparing to write to you about the
salvation we share,
I find it necessary to write and appeal to you
to contend for the faith
that was once and for all handed on to the saints."
(Jude 3, NRSVUE)

A scene from the award-winning movie *Titanic* encapsulates the cultural captivity of this season in North America. It takes place early in the movie as the passengers are boarding the mighty ocean liner. Staring up at the *Titanic* with awestruck excitement, a passenger comments, "this is a ship so mighty that not even God can sink it." A shade under five days later the mighty vessel, already half submerged and almost perpendicular to the water, plunged to her grave 2.4 miles deep in the Atlantic.

Contrary to popular belief, it was not a head-on blow with sunk the *Titanic*. Her end came from a slashing tear delivered by a part of the iceberg which couldn't even be seen below the waterline. This is a cautionary tale that offers apprehensive insight into the ripping apart of the United Methodist Church.

In my letter of withdrawal from the Council of Bishops and the United Methodist Church, I (Bishop Mike Lowry) stated: "Regretfully, I perceive that the institutional expression of The United

Methodist Church has strayed in significant ways from faithfully upholding its stated *Discipline* and, even more so, departed from the full truth of the gospel." The presenting issue is characterized by a dispute over our understanding of human sexuality, more specifically whether or not clergy should be allowed to perform same-gender marriages and whether it is permissible to ordain "self-avowed practicing homosexuals." Our strong contention is that the presenting issue masks the deeper and truly significant disagreement over what constitutes fidelity to the historic confession of the Christian faith. We wish to highlight six crucial areas of disagreement, five primarily theological in content and the sixth organizational, which constitute the grounds of our contending for the faith «that was once and for all handed on to the saints."[20]

1. The nature and role of the authority of Holy Scripture

2. The nature and role of Jesus Christ, fully human and fully divine (the Chalcedonian definition)

3. The nature and role of sin

4. The nature and role of salvation (doctrine of atonement)

5. The nature and role of sanctification ("saved to the uttermost")

6. The United Methodist Church has become ungovernable.

The historic faith is expressed in the normative nature of Holy Scripture as the primary rule of faith, the ecumenical creeds, the Articles of Religion, and Wesley's Standard Sermons.

Built on the aforementioned deep theological grounds, the crucial sixth reason is functionally ecclesiological. The United Methodist Church as currently constituted has become ungovernable. Janice Huie, retired United Methodist Bishop and former President of the UMC Council of Bishops, has stated that the United Methodist Church is a "spider caught in its own web." Viewed as a whole, we find the Wesleyan movement contending for the very heart of the Christian faith and for church governance (ecclesiology) that faithfully enacts the Wesleyan understanding of Christ's church.

The presenting issue is starkly before us, as laid out in chapter one, in straightforward terms which revolve around an understanding of a doctrine of creation and repeated biblical admonitions about proper behavior. To modern ears, especially those educated and nurtured in a culture governed by the desires and will of the (supposed) sovereign individual, Christian claims which take seriously biblical admonitions such as Paul's statement against "dishonorable passions"[21] in Romans sound strangely out of touch. Yet the presenting issue over same-gender marriage and ordination of "avowed practicing homosexuals"[22] for Christian churches rises before us as the tip of a much larger iceberg threatening to gut the church of Jesus Christ, much like an iceberg sliced into the *Titanic* a little over 110 years ago and sent the once great ship to its death.

The struggle over truth is not a new one for the Christian faith. The great ecumenical councils and the Apostles and Nicaean creeds were outgrowths of the larger struggle over just what was and is Christian and what is not. Heresy in all its many forms is not simply an errant belief that should be treated with bemused tolerance and a gentle pat on the head. Heresy is diseased Christianity which must be gracefully yet firmly confronted in any age and time. Alister McGrath defines heresy this way: "A heresy is a doctrine that ultimately destroys, destabilizes, or distorts a mystery rather than preserving it."[23]

Seen in the context of the separation developing within the United Methodist Church, some view the liberalization of sexual ethics and associated commitment to what is called full inclusion as both liberating and holy. Yet, far from a narrow-minded attempt to "keep the church pure", the struggle over core doctrines involves the health and vitality of the church. Behind the good intentions of full inclusion lies a distorting and even destructive bent to human willfulness over God's creative design. Core doctrines [teachings] of creation, sanctification, and ultimately the Lordship of Christ are at stake. The challenge before us is: Will we follow the one who alone is Lord or displace his rule with our preferences however noble and well-intended?

By way of examining the deeper theological issue, the massive iceberg beneath the surface of today's Methodist expression of church faithfulness, we invite the reader to a careful examination of an often-forgotten letter in the back of the New Testament. The searing words of the second paragraph of the letter of Jude both frame and highlight a fight for the Christian faith taking place beneath the waterline of the looming separation of the Global Methodist Church from The United Methodist Church. "Dear friends, I wanted very much to write to you concerning the salvation we share. Instead, I must write to urge you to fight for the faith delivered once and for all to God's holy people. Godless people have slipped in among you. They turn the grace of our God into unrestrained immorality and deny our only Master and Lord, Jesus Christ. Judgment was passed against them a long time ago."[24]

The match was lit to this theological and spiritual powder keg at the very inception of The United Methodist Church. The First Restrictive Rule of the Constitution of the newly instituted church clearly stated (and still states): "The General Conference shall not revoke, alter, or change our Articles of Religion or establish any new standards or rules of doctrine contrary to our present existing and established standards of doctrines."[25] Yet concomitant with such a commitment to doctrinal clarity has been great confusion as to precisely what the standards are, what they mean, and how they might in some way be enforced.

The fire was stoked and brought to a roaring blaze with the adoption of the *1972 Book of Discipline of the United Methodist Church*, officially advocating doctrinal pluralism. The resulting theological chaos has led to theological instability at the heart of the United Methodist denomination. Despite a clear re-forming of doctrinal standards by United Methodists in the 1988 General Conference, much of the doctrinal preaching and teaching by United Methodist pastors reflect a vague pluralism tinctured with Unitarianism and a rejection of the very notion of a theological standard to which ordained United Methodists must adhere.

In earlier writing for *Firebrand,* I (Bishop Lowry) shared several anecdotal illustrations. These bear repeating here, for both of us have experienced similar incidents. The first came in a conversation with a highly regarded retired clergyperson in a public setting.

This man had been a serious episcopal candidate. We were discussing what doctrinal convictions were required for ordination.

I [Bishop Lowry] queried, "Would you vote for a candidate for ordination who did not believe in the Trinity; someone who was essentially a unitarian?"

He paused and noticeably thought for a moment. Then he slowly nodded. "Yes, yes I would."

Consider the implications of such a statement. At the very heart of the Nicene-Chalcedonian understanding of the Christian faith is the doctrine of the Holy Trinity. The United Methodist Church holds in its Articles of Religion (which are constituted as its core ruling doctrine) a non-negotiable trinitarian commitment. "Article I – Of Faith in the Holy Trinity: there is but one living and true God, everlasting, without body or parts, of infinite wisdom and goodness; the maker and preserver of all things, both visible and invisible. And in the unity of this Godhead, there are three persons of one substance, power, and eternity – the Father, the Son, and the Holy Ghost."

Another incident took place in a conversation between district superintendents. [The district superintendent (DS) is a significant middle-judicatory supervision role in The United Methodist Church which is formally an extension of the episcopal office.] In a discussion bordering upon an argument with other district superintendents, one prominent DS asserted that talk of crucifixion should be jettisoned. She stated, "we have to stop preaching that Jesus died on the cross for us… it does damage to people." Another agreed and argued further that "here [in communion] should not be any confessional language at all." He went on to say, "We have to stop making people feel guilty and like they need to confess sins when they come to church. We aren't Catholic."

As the comments were shared, all I could think of was the Apostle Paul's clarion conviction of faith: "But we preach Christ crucified, which is a scandal to Jews and foolishness to Gentiles."

A third anecdotal incident I shared took place in a recent conversation with the senior pastor of a large church in my conference, we reflected together on our mission statement, "to make disciples of Jesus Christ for the transformation of the world." This man, who has been a delegate to General Conference and served in a leadership position on the Board of Ordained Ministry (the credentialing body for candidates for ordination), argued that we need to leave out the part about Jesus Christ and emphasize the "transformation of the world." Christology was to him, at best, a minor sideline. Further discussion revealed that he perceived Jesus as a great teacher but could not affirm the Chalcedonian understanding of Christ. The second major element of doctrinal contention we have lifted– The nature and role of Jesus Christ, fully human and fully divine – was for him a discernable aspect of being Christian.

Once again, I could not help but think of the earliest Christians' three-word creedal commitment: "Jesus is Lord." The courageously soaring statement of Philippians 2:6-11 echoed in my pained heart "that at the name of Jesus everyone in heaven, on earth, and under the earth might bow and every tongue confess that Jesus Christ is Lord, to the glory of God the Father."[26]

To these incidents, we invite the readers to consider the evidence from three of the United Methodist Church's thirteen official seminaries.

Claremont School of Theology in California publicly considers itself to no longer be a Christian seminary! Instead, it lifts high its commitment to interfaith ministry. It holds to this conviction even while accepting a substantial amount of money from the United Methodist Church's "Ministerial Education Fund" (MEF) as one of the UMC's thirteen official seminaries. There is no mention of Christ and the United Methodist Church's mission to "make disciples of Jesus Christ" in its public mission statement.[27]

Iliff School of Theology in Denver likewise makes no mention of Christ or the Christian mission to "make disciples of Jesus Christ" in its public "Purpose and Vision" statement. It is difficult to find any explicitly Christian reference to ordained ministry on its website.[28] Once again, a substantial portion of Iliff's finances come from the United Methodist Church's Ministerial Education Fund via the denomination's General Board of Higher Education and Ministry.

Lest we casually dismiss this as simply a "western" (both Claremont and Iliff are in the ardently progressive liberal Western Jurisdiction of the United Methodist Church) expression of the United Methodist Church, consider Methodist Theological School in Ohio (MTSO) which is located near Columbus, Ohio in the center of the state. Once again there is no mention of "Christ" or the Christian mission "to make disciples of Jesus Christ for the transformation of the world" on their mission page. MTSO does however lift its Unitarian House of Study program. In fairness, MTSO does affirm its "Christian identity as a seminary in the Wesleyan family" buried in a longer document on their strategic plan. It highlights "Sustainable justice" as their "central institutional commitment" but there is no mention of such a laudable commitment being anchored in Christ.[29]

While it is difficult to precisely document the degree of denominational drift from a core Christian commitment to Jesus Christ as Lord and the mission of making "disciples of Jesus Christ for the transformation of the world" among United Methodist clergy, our experience as a bishop, chair of a Board of Ordained Ministry and membership on two different Boards of Ordained Ministry have provided extensive first-hand experience in the clergy "trenches" of United Methodism. I (Bishop Lowry) earlier chaired the old Southwest Texas Conference's Board of Ordained Ministry, and Dr. Greenway served a combined 22 years on Western Pennsylvania and West Ohio Conference Boards of Ministry as well as supervisory ministry as a District Superintendent. Additionally, we have served as delegates to a combined eight General Conferences—and as professors, administrators, and trustees in United Methodist Seminaries. Together our combined 73+ years as ordained clergy in the UMC have led us to believe that the problem of doctrinal drift from the core of the Christian faith is substantial.

One element of doctrinal disagreement is often the use of common language with very different meanings attached to the words used. Two examples illustrate the problem.

While there is a general acknowledgment of the importance of Jesus, orthodox Christianity has robustly affirmed the understanding contained in the Nicene Creed and confirmed by the Council of Chalcedon that Jesus Christ is "fully human" and "fully divine." Many, if not most, who align with a progressive view of Christian theology hold that Jesus is a man, perhaps divinely inspired, but still a human subject to error and not God truly and fully incarnate. Such an understanding denies the reality of John 1:14, "And the Word became flesh and lived among us, and we have seen his glory, the glory as of a father's only son, full of grace and truth."[30] In doing so, an ax is laid to the tree of salvation and a doctrine of atonement is subsumed into a vague universalism. Jesus no longer saves us from the ravages of sin and death but merely points the way to being better humans.

A second example strikes at the heart of Paul's clarion assertion that "if Christ has not been raised, then our proclamation is in vain and your faith is in vain."[31] A gathering of the clergy will all acknowledge belief in the resurrection of Jesus, but clarifying questions will reveal that while some believe and affirm the resurrection to be a physical, bodily resurrection of Jesus from death to life in Jerusalem in the early First Century as described in the Gospels, testified to throughout the New Testament, and affirmed in the earliest creeds of the Church; others will see the resurrection as a metaphor or an allegory. It would not be difficult to cite similar examples about creation, miracles, the authoritative reliability of the Scripture, and the nature of divine revelation.

Looking at the evidence gathered, when taken as a whole, Jude's claim that we must "contend for the faith once delivered" rings true as a clarion call directed at today's Methodist movement. Our contention is straightforward. The United Methodist Church as it is currently constituted has lost much of its theological core. We are paying the price today for generations of pastors and seminary teachers having ignored core doctrines of the Christian faith. Like Jude, we would wish to write about the salvation we share, but instead are convicted of the need to "contend [or fight] for the faith delivered once for all." However harsh it may seem, "Godless people have slipped in among [us]." Disguised in the form of pluralism and tolerance we have embraced doctrinal indifference. With such an embrace has come the destructive chaos of cheap grace turned into "unrestrained immorality" which denies "our only Master and Lord, Jesus Christ" (Jude4).

Advice to Jude is advice for us as well. Scholars debate precisely what was meant by "godless people" in Jude's day. Likely, those so labeled "godless" saw themselves as good and even godly. There is reason to believe they were upholding a vision of grace that freed them from a doctrine of sin. As N. T. Wright and Michael F. Bird put it, "They deny the moral implications of the gospel, thereby effectively denying the authority of Jesus himself."[32] At stake is a sound understanding of the nature and role of sin as previously noted.

The application of Jude's label of "godless people" appears unduly harsh in today's permissive theological climate. It carries implications of harsh judgmentalism. Yet once again Jude would instruct us: judgment is real. "Judgment was passed against them a long time ago." His argument about judgment takes up the major part of this letter. As Alister McGrath argues in *Heresy: A History of Defending the Truth*, false teaching is best seen as a form of diseased Christianity. Jude's harsh label serves as a warning that doctrinal indifferentism too long tolerated and even embraced leads to "godlessness."

In our day, the disease that infects us, while disguised as kind non-judgmentalism, brings destructive consequences. Those who advocate an expansive view of grace to leech out the moral implications of the gospel no doubt believe they are faithfully reflecting divine grace. "Godless people" may have good intentions, but we should be well advised that the "road to hell is paved with good intentions." Application to early 21st century North America should not be avoided. The philosophical climate of radical individualism in American culture (and The United Methodist Church), combined with a hedonistic addiction to the pursuit of personal pleasure, salted with partisan invective, and soaked in personal arrogance is leading the church far from submission to Jesus as Lord.

The doctrine of permissive cheap grace evident in much of The United Methodist Church's current theological stance is ultimately destructive to individuals and the church itself. Likewise, the tendency to slip into a denial of the fullness of Jesus Christ (fully human, fully divine) carries with it the ultimate weakening of the very moral attributes offered by a Savior who calls us to holy living. Our Lord's teaching is not just one opinion among many. Orthodox Christology as promulgated by the Nicene Creed matters.

One of the giants of the Christian faith in America in the last half of the 20th century and the first part of the 21st century was Richard John Neuhaus. Originally a Lutheran clergy, Neuhaus later became a Roman Catholic priest and was a founder of the influential ecumenical journal *First Things*. Neuhaus laid out what has come to be known simply as "Neuhaus's Law." It states: "Where orthodoxy is optional, orthodoxy will sooner or later be proscribed."[33] He went on to explain why orthodoxy cannot be just one option among many.

> "Orthodoxy, no matter how politely expressed, suggests that there is a right and a wrong, a true and a false, about things. When orthodoxy is optional, it is admitted under a rule of liberal tolerance that cannot help but be intolerant of talk about right and wrong, true and false. It is therefore a conditional admission, depending upon orthodoxy's good behavior. The orthodox may be permitted to believe this or that and to do this or that as a matter of sufferance, allowing them to indulge their inclination, preference, or personal taste. But it is an intolerable violation of the etiquette by which one is tolerated if one has the effrontery to propose that this or that is normative for others.[34]

Currently, we are seeing this reality unfold in the Wesleyan movement.

The current dispute in The United Methodist Church is largely a battle over where Christians draw the line of faith (if they draw a line of faith at all!). It bears repeating. The presenting issues of whether clergy should be allowed to perform same-gender marriages and whether it is permissible to ordain "self-avowed practicing homosexuals" are the proverbial tip of the iceberg in the "fight for the faith delivered once and for all." The massive iceberg beneath the water is the ongoing argument over just what constitutes the theological and moral foundations of contemporary Methodism.

One fascinating example of this lies in the contentious debate in The United Methodist Church over just where the doctrinal and moral lines should be drawn. In our experience, we have dealt with many who advocate an understanding of grace that will cover almost any behavior without repentance or a behavior change. When pressed as to where a line might be drawn in terms of understanding sin, we often encounter a refusal or an intellectual inability to articulate any doctrinal (and often few moral) boundary lines. Pertinently, Kenda Creasy Dean has stated, "Arguably, issues of identity and openness pose the most daunting challenges facing American Christianity in the twenty-first century." She went on to query, "Where is the line between identity and openness?"[35]

The antinomian convictions of modern society that have infected the church are consistently failing people. The spiritual hunger we encounter, while often embedded in a radical individual hedonism, is a sign of a desperate search for something better, something deeper. Perceptively Professor Dean remarks, "Perhaps young people lack robust Christian identities because churches offer such a stripped-down version of Christianity that it no longer poses a viable alternative to imposter spiritualties like Moralistic Therapeutic Deism."[36] (see Chapter 6 on the Battle with Moralistic Therapeutic Deism.)

In the witness shared in Jude's opening, we encounter again the outlines of a vibrant orthodoxy that can survive the diseased Christianity of our time. Jude offers us a place to stand in the "fight for a faith delivered once for all." Jude challenges us in three ways to rediscover radical allegiance to Jesus Christ as Lord, recognize reality, and reclaim orthodoxy.

First, Jude can assert a family connection through James to Jesus himself. His pedigree is impeccable. Instead of making such a claim, Jude connects his teaching authority to Jesus Christ. He is "a slave of Jesus Christ" (v. 1). Later in the letter, he drives home this cardinal conviction of his relationship: "our onlyMaster and Lord, Jesus Christ" (v.4). It is here our fight for the faith must begin. The letter of Jude is a passionate call for modern Christians to rediscover radical allegiance to Jesus Christ as Lord. Bluntly put, the Methodist movement must reclaim the central place of allegiance to Jesus Christ as our only master and Lord over and above the standards of secular culture.

In a perceptive piece of writing, Matthew Bates notes that our understanding of the word "faith" has become diminished over time. "The Greek word *Pistis*, generally rendered 'faith' or 'belief,' as it pertains to Christian salvation, quite simply has little correlation with 'faith' and 'belief' as these words are generally understood and used in contemporary Christian culture, and much to do with allegiance. At the center of Christianity properly understood is not the human response of faith or belief but rather the old-fashioned term *fidelity*."[37]

Jude's strong affirmation of the Lordship of Christ challenges us to submit our preferences to His purpose. Theologically speaking, the fight for the faith delivered once to all is anchored to a foundation of reclaiming Chalcedon Christology and the concept of radical allegiance. Again, Bates comments, "Jesus as the universal Lord is the primary object toward which our saving 'faith' – that is, our saving allegiance is directed. We must stop asking others to invite Jesus into their hearts and start asking them to swear allegiance to Jesus the king."[38]

Second, Jude calls us to face reality. Consider for a moment that as the brother of James (and thus a brother of Jesus) all the things Jude might well have written about. He tells us at the start of his letter that his preference was to write about "salvation." Instead, Jude understands the context of his day. He recognized the reality of his time. In our time, the temptation is to be consumed by concerns for institutional connection and possible schism rather than face the deeper doctrinal issue before us. We could legitimately spend time writing about the various institutional and individually moral issues confronting society – racism, sexism, violence, war, environmental challenges, etc. Jude was contending with a rapacious Roman Empire built on slavery and violence. Yet Jude perceived the greater threat to the heart of the gospel was false teaching. We must do the same in this day and time. He would teach us not to hide from the reality of our time but confront the theological poverty of our day with the truth of the gospel.

In recognizing this reality, Wright and Bird pointedly connect Jude's insight with the church of today: "Parts of the Christian church today seem ideationally vacuous, with little or no confessional content to their faith. They tend also to be places where manifold forms of immorality are permitted and even celebrated. In such a context, we are to contend for the faith without being contentious over tertiary matters."[39] As Christendom fades into the cultural background, it is time to wake up to the reality of our need to contend for the Christian faith.

Third, Jude calls us to reclaim orthodoxy. Significantly he speaks of the "faith once delivered," not of a new or expanded personal interpretation. Jude does not engage in a culturally popular proclamation. His scriptural references are tough and to the point. "But you, dear friends, remember the words spoken beforehand by the apostles of our Lord Jesus Christ."[40] Without apology, he reclaims the connection of theology with moral practice.

Our modern failure in much of the church to hold to the historic theological core of the Christian faith erodes our very ability to speak to the moral anarchy of our times. For far too many, Christian theological and ethical commitments have been reduced to matters of opinion and political advocacy. It is past time to reclaim the heart of the gospel against the raging hedonism and selfishness of our age.

C. S. Lewis's warning almost three-quarters of a century ago to a group of young Anglican priests and youth workers still holds today:

> "I insist that wherever you draw the lines, bounding lines must exist, beyond which your doctrines will cease to be Anglican or to be Christian; and I suggest also that the lines come a great deal sooner than many modern priests think. I think it is your duty to fix the lines clearly in your own minds: and if you wish to go beyond them you must change your profession. This is your duty not specifically as Christians or as priests but honest men…. We are to defend Christianity itself—the faith preached by the Apostles, attested by the

Martyrs, embodied in the Creeds, expounded by the Fathers. This must be clearly distinguished from the whole of what any one of us may think about God and man...."[41]

In the six basis points of disagreement which stand behind the presenting issue, we are contending for the faith delivered once and for all. The struggle over the future of The United Methodist Church and the dawn of the Global Methodist Church involves no less than a rediscovery, recognition, and reclaiming of the historic roots of the Methodist movement at the heart of the Christian faith. The time of theological toleration saturated with moral indifference is past. The reality before us is of a diseased Christianity that we must counter by rediscovering radical allegiance to Christ, recognizing the reality of the battle we are in, and reclaiming core Christian orthodoxy. Here, at the dawn of a new church, a new Wesleyan expression of the historic orthodox Christian church compels us to "contend for the faith that was once and for all handed on to the saints."[42]

To this end, we pray the benediction of Jude.

"To the one who is able to protect you from falling,
and to present you blameless and rejoicing before his glorious presence,
to the only God our Savior, through Jesus Christ our Lord,
belong glory, majesty, power, and authority,
before all time, now and forever. Amen."[43]

CHAPTER 3:
WHY WE NEED TO SEPARATE

*"But mark this: There will be terrible times in the
last days. People will be lovers of themselves, lovers of
money, boastful, proud, abusive, disobedient to their
parents, ungrateful, unholy, without love, unforgiving,
slanderous, without self-control, brutal, not lovers of the
good, treacherous, rash, conceited, lovers of pleasure rather
than lovers of God— having a form of godliness but denying its power. Have nothing to do with such people."*
2 Timothy 3:1-5 (NIV)

*"I am not afraid that the people called Methodists should
ever cease to exist either in Europe or America. But I am
afraid, lest they should only exist as a dead sect, having the
form of religion without the power. And this undoubtedly
will be the case, unless they hold fast both the doctrine,
spirit, and discipline with which they first set out."*
(John Wesley in Thoughts on Methodism—
August 4, 1786)

We believe in the Church. We know some folks believe the
work being done to separate from the United Methodist
Church and launch the Global Methodist Church is the ecclesial equivalent of "high crimes and misdemeanors;" and that those
who've anticipated and planned for separation are seen as treason-
ous. But we believe in the Church.

However, the Church isn't a building, a social club, a preaching center, or even a denomination. It's the embodiment of Jesus' life and love in the world today. The church is a group of people who know Jesus and exist to lead other people to Jesus. We're not saved to isolation and individualism. God intends for salvation to be a community-creating event. We need the church. It's in community that we grow to our greatest potential.

The question is: what "church" are we talking about? When talking about the church, we need to distinguish between the "little c" church and the "big C" Church. The "big C" Church is the Church of Jesus Christ. It was born of the Spirit on Pentecost and comprises all the "little c" churches—past, present, and future. The United Methodist Church and the Global Methodist Church are "little c" churches which are only small parts of the "big C" Church. "Little c" churches like these are only significant to the extent they're contributing to the mission of the "big C" Church. The "big C" Church transcends apparent dichotomies like Catholic and Protestant, Baptist and Methodist, traditional and contemporary, clergy and laity, priests and pastors, dunkers and sprinklers, ordained and licensed, and the various theological camps. The "big C" Church reaches across time and space and holds firm even as empires rise and fall. The "big C" Church is bigger than you; bigger than us; bigger than all of us.

Fueled and Driven by the Holy Spirit

The Church is a movement fueled and driven by the Holy Spirit. In John 16, Jesus was talking with his disciples the night before his crucifixion when he said, "It is better for you that I go away, because if I don't, the advocate (paraclete) won't come."[44] The Greek word "paraclete" means "called to one's side to encourage, uphold, assist, and help." The Holy Spirit is a helper sent to encourage, uphold, and assist the Church as we lift the cause of the Kingdom of God. Later that night, Jesus was arrested, beaten, and condemned. The next day, Jesus was crucified, dead, and buried. And on the third day, Jesus rose from the dead. The Gospel of John ends with the risen and living Jesus appearing to his disciples.

On the next page, in the Acts of the Apostles chapter 1, forty days after the resurrection, Jesus told his disciples, "Do not leave Jerusalem until the Father sends you what he promised. Remember I have told you about this before. John baptized with water, but in just a few days I will baptize you with the Holy Spirit."[45] Jesus was leaving the earth so the Holy Spirit would come. The disciples stayed in Jerusalem. They waited and prayed. Ten days later, their prayer meeting was interrupted by the "sound of a rushing wind" and the Holy Spirit arrived in the form of tongues of fire settling upon the people in the room. At that moment, the "big C" Church was born.

As we read the Acts of the Apostles, it becomes clear the person of Jesus, who was limited by his physical body, is now gone, and he has sent the unlimited Holy Spirit in his place. The Holy Spirit was everywhere at once, and the era of the Spirit-filled Church began. Acts chapter 4 gives us a glimpse of what it was like, "All the believers were of one heart and mind, they shared their possessions, and the Apostles gave powerful witness to the resurrection of the Lord. And God's great favor was on them all."[46]

And they all lived happily ever after, right? Wrong! Acts chapter 5 opens with the story of Ananias and Sapphira who were struck dead because they lied to the Holy Spirit. Acts chapter 6 shows factions of the Church fighting over the fair distribution of food to their widows. Isn't it fascinating that the first two problems to hit the fledgling Church were hypocrisy and injustice? We are so glad we don't have problems like that today!

The rest of the New Testament tells the dynamic story of the Church which most historians believe grew from 120 people at Pentecost to hundreds of thousands in fifty years. Yet, despite great success in spreading the Gospel, an unsettling undercurrent runs throughout the New Testament: There are problems in the Church. Some come from the outside (that's expected), but the most serious are those that come from within. That's troubling, but it still happens today. Which raises the question: If the Church is God's plan to carry out the ministry of Jesus, why is it so messed up? The short answer is because it's filled with people—like us!

For the last several years, the "little c" United Methodist Church has been in a time of open schism and crisis. Many of us believe that parts of our "little c" church have exemplified what Paul instructs to Timothy: *"Preach the word; be prepared in season and out of season; correct, rebuke and encourage—with great patience and careful instruction. For the time will come when people will not put up with sound doctrine. Instead, to suit their own desires, they will gather around them a great number of teachers to say what their itching ears want to hear. They will turn their ears away from the truth and turn aside to myths. But you, keep your head in all situations, endure hardship, do the work of an evangelist, discharge all the duties of your ministry."*[47]

The Need for Separation

The foundation for our theological crisis has been in place since the very beginning when we embraced the grand experiment of theological pluralism, resulting in a sort of "big tent" Methodism where a variety of theological expressions were valued. There was a sense of mutual appreciation and tolerance at that time. I (Jeff Greenway) can remember talking with some of my older, more liberal colleagues who would not agree with my more orthodox perspectives, but they would say there was room in their church for me. It was a generous pluralism whose limits had not yet been truly tested. Those limits are now being tested because our theological pluralism has stressed and crumbled the biblical and theological foundations of our "little c" church. That kind of theological generosity is no longer possible when there is no common doctrinal foundation or when the agreed-upon denominational covenant lay in the rubble.

A cursory reading of Christian history reveals the occasional need for followers of Jesus to separate and even multiply their expressions of Christian faith. Often, it has been to further the Kingdom. The Methodist Movement began as a reform movement in the Church of England but separated itself from the Church of England for a variety of strategic missional reasons.

We believe separations are sometimes necessary and even justified if the motivation is for the sake of the mission of making disciples of Jesus Christ.[48] If this is the criteria, we are in good company. At the end of the Acts of the Apostles chapter 15, Paul and Barnabas had just secured the blessing of the Jerusalem Council to take the Gospel to the Gentiles and were preparing to leave on their second missionary journey from Antioch. At this pivotal moment in the Christian movement, Paul and Barnabas had a sharp disagreement over John Mark. Barnabas, the "son of encouragement," wanted to give his cousin, John Mark, a second chance and take him along. Paul didn't. He'd had enough of John Mark—he'd left the first missionary journey because he became homesick. This disagreement had the potential to derail the mission—stopping it dead in its tracks.

However, Paul and Barnabas refused to allow their disagreement to derail the mission. Paul took Silas and went off to missionary fame. Barnabas took John Mark, and we never hear about Barnabas again. However, Barnabas did what he did best—he poured his life into helping John Mark answer God's call.

One of the most remarkable things about the story is what happened to John Mark. He became Simon Peter's traveling companion and eventually wrote the Gospel of Mark. Later, Paul wrote Timothy and told him to bring Mark with him because he was now helpful to him.[49] Paul also wrote about Mark (the cousin of Barnabas) being with him while he was under house arrest awaiting trial in Rome.[50]

Here's the point: Paul and Barnabas went their separate ways instead of jeopardizing the mission. We contend we're at a Paul and Barnabas moment in our tradition, and we shouldn't allow our inner squabbling to prevent us from pursuing the mission which may be better served if we bless each other and separate. We're excited to see what God does when pursuing the mission once again becomes central.

I (Jeff Greenway) believe we need to separate. This wasn't an easy conclusion for me to reach. Methodism is the spiritual root from which my family's heritage of faith has grown. I'm a second-generation United Methodist clergyperson. I love the church. Bishop Lowry came to United Methodism through a different path, but he loves the church as well. We've spent most of our adult lives trying to reform and renew our "little c" church to align with and be faithful to the "big C" Church; but every act of ecclesial disobedience, every incidence of ignoring our common covenant, and every provocative act by those in authority has helped me (Jeff Greenway) realize this isn't my father's United Methodist Church. Nor is it the covenant community into which either one of us was ordained. We firmly believe it is time to separate.

During the last several years, we've used our time to fulfill the ministries to which we've been appointed or assigned and to be actively engaged in praying, dreaming, and planning for the launch of the Global Methodist Church. We've prayed and planned. We've prayed and strategized. We've prayed and negotiated. We've prayed and acted in faith and integrity. We've prayed and done everything we can do to find a way to amicably separate from a denomination that has lost its way.

As we write, we stand at a significant point in time. Some institutionalist United Methodists make the appeal that our differences are not significant enough to merit separation. They advocate that we're better together and promise that no one will have to compromise their core beliefs or principles in the utopic future they envision. We disagree. Prior collective history says this is not possible. We believe we need to separate. We are no longer better together.

Six Reasons Why Separation is Necessary

1. We are No Longer Governable

There is nothing wrong with our present United Methodist polity and discipline or the official doctrines of the church, but the lack of fidelity to and compliance with our agreed-upon system of governance and polity has led us to a constitutional crisis. Those charged with leading the church and holding us accountable can't hold one another accountable. The move toward regionalization of belief and practice has placed us in a time like the book of Judges where "everyone does what's wise in their own eyes."[51] The result is broken trust and covenant.

We write as veterans of the United Methodist Church at every level. During multiple General Conferences, we have learned it doesn't matter how many times the General Conference acts to affirm or attempts to hold us accountable to our covenants; we are ungovernable as long as some bishops, Conferences, and Jurisdictions act as a law unto themselves and refuse to abide by our commonly agreed upon system of governance. Our system is broken and ungovernable.

2. We have a Language Problem

The words we use to express who we are and what we believe in the church don't mean the same thing to everyone using them. For the last several years, I've contended that the challenge facing us is that we use the same words, cite the same scriptures, quote the same Wesley sermons, and pledge fidelity to the same *Book of Discipline*, but because we don't have a common understanding of what the words mean—we're living entirely different expressions of the faith. It's increasingly difficult to find a common language upon which to agree, and as a result, we don't understand each other.

For example, if we were to use the word "resurrection" those hearing us could assume we meant that the incarnate Son of God, Jesus, who lived a perfect life and died an atoning death for the sins of the world on the cross was buried in a borrowed tomb outside of Jerusalem at the beginning of the Passover Festival in 30 AD—and was physically raised from the dead three days later. This is a matter of essential and basic faith for us, but we have colleagues who have a very different view. Jesus is not seen as the incarnate Son of God, the atonement is described as child abuse and dismissed as unnecessary, and the resurrection is viewed as allegory. We all use the name Jesus and say we believe in the resurrection but have very different understandings of the words.

3. We have very different theologies

This is, in part, because of our language problem. Many in the United Methodist world believe we're divided by differing views on human sexuality. We disagree. Human sexuality is only the presenting symptom. The real cause of our division is rooted in fundamental differences in some of the core doctrines of the church. Let us give you a few examples:

a. **We disagree on the nature, role, and authority of Scripture**, and our differing approaches to interpretation begin and end in entirely different places. Some of us believe the Bible is the word of God. Others contend it contains the word of God. Some believe the canon is closed. Others believe "new revelation" takes precedence over the biblical canon. Some believe the entire Bible is true and authoritative. Others believe it can be divided into three categories (or "buckets") and portions can be dismissed as non-authoritative. Some believe our experience is to be subject to Scripture. Others believe our experience is more important than and therefore supersedes Scripture.

b. **We also disagree on the nature, role, and authority of Jesus.** Some believe in the incarnation, virgin birth, physical death, and bodily resurrection of Jesus as described in Scripture and affirmed in the Apostles and Nicene Creeds. Others don't and cross their fingers when being questioned and examined for ordination. Friends, either Jesus is who He said He is and did everything He said He would do, or we have nothing life-changing to offer the world.

c. **We disagree on the nature of sin and its needed atonement.** Some believe sin is personal, that it separates us from a relationship with God, needs to be atoned for, and is forgiven when we place our faith in the life, death, and resurrection of Jesus. To quote our friend, Shane Bishop, "Sin will beg to be tolerated, ask to be accepted and then demand to be celebrated. It's what sin does." Others don't want to hear about, and sometimes act to minimize personal sin. Others believe human beings are inherently good, and sin is corrected solely through acts of justice and mercy. Modern Methodists have disconnected two things that John Wesley held in tension: the absolute need for a saving relationship with Jesus and the very out-growth of that relationship—changed lives that then change communities and cultures.

d. **We disagree on the meaning of justification or salvation.** Some of us believe in the absolute necessity of Wesley's teaching on the Scripture Way of Salvation including conviction, repentance, justification, conversion, new birth, adoption, and assurance of salvation on a personal basis. We must be born again. Others view salvation as a universal civil right and see no real need to call others to repentance and salvation.

e. **We disagree on the ongoing work of sanctification or Christian Perfection.** Some see sanctification as the work of the Holy Spirit that continues saving us from sin and delivering us into new life. We're not only saved from the penalty of our sin but we can also be delivered from its power and control over our lives. Others resist the continuing work of the Spirit in pointing out the residue of sin and its effect on our lives and shun or deny the need to be what Wesley called being "saved to the uttermost."

These differing theological perspectives once resided happily under the covering of "big tent" Methodism, but the lack of a theological center and the continued, deliberate moving of the stakes of the progressive side of the tent toward ideologies we dare to say are not even Christian, have torn the fabric of the "big tent." Theologically speaking, we're coming apart at the seams.

4. We don't want to be in the same church.
We might say we do, but because of our language problems and deep theological differences, we often behave badly toward those who oppose us. This cuts both ways. When power dynamics go unchecked, the fact that we don't trust or want to be in the same church with each other becomes clearer. There are regions in the United Methodist Church that haven't had any orthodox leadership in decades—if ever. The same could be said by someone progressive in more orthodox regions.

Some places, like where I (Jeff Greenway) serve in West Ohio, that are more theologically diverse have seen the civility of the past disappear over the last decade. Recent denominational headlines about provocative changes in pastoral appointments to orthodox congregations, the firing or forced resignations of orthodox faculty members at United Methodist seminaries, and increasing intolerance toward evangelical, orthodox United Methodists by persons of different theologies, are all leading indicators of intolerance coming toward evangelicals in the present or post-separation United Methodist Church.

5. We're hurting each other.

The fifty-four-year history of the United Methodist Church is littered with the causalities of the harm caused by our inability to resolve our conflict and hold one another accountable. The wounded can be found on both sides of our divide. We've tolerated the casualties because of our belief in and loyalty to the institution.

As students of leadership and organizations, we've learned a very important lesson about institutions—they exist to protect themselves. When an institution (or those charged with protecting it) is threatened, it will do whatever is necessary to preserve itself—even to the point of breaking its own rules and violating its ethos to silence dissent and contrary views. Loss is calculated, retrenchment and organizational reforms are attempted, and individuals are often sacrificed on the altar of institutional preservation. These patterns accelerate as the threat increases. Over the years, our effort to preserve our institution has caused irreparable harm. It is time to stop hurting each other—and find a way to bless and send each other.

6. We need to start planting

The Old Testament prophets Isaiah and Micah foretold a time when God's people would beat their swords into plowshares. It was a reminder the day would come to stop fighting and start planting again. During the 50+ years of our existence as a denomination, we've learned how to fight with each other. We've developed finely tuned machinery for waging ecclesiastical war. The fighting hasn't only scarred the soul of our church, it has damaged our social witness to the world around us. Each negative headline or social media skirmish only serves to further damage our witness and stain our reputation. We need to free one another to pursue the separate and competing visions of our preferred futures.

For these reasons and more, we believe separation is necessary. We take no joy in finding ourselves at this juncture, but we're not without hope. We write to remind us all that this is not the first time people who claim the name of Jesus have separated. What began with Paul and Barnabas has happened repeatedly over time, often to the good of the surviving parts of the separation. We'll address this in the next chapter.

1	WE ARE NO LONGER GOVERNABLE
2	WE HAVE A LANGUAGE PROBLEM
3	WE HAVE VERY DIFFERENT THEOLOGIES
4	WE DON'T WANT TO BE IN THE SAME CHURCH
5	WE ARE HURTING EACH OTHER
6	WE NEED TO START PLANTING

CHAPTER 4:
THE LORD OF HISTORY

*"Therefore the Lord the God of Israel declares: ‹I promised
that your family and the family of your ancestor should go
in and out before me forever, but now the Lord declares:
Far be it from me, for those who honor me I will honor,
and those who despise me shall be treated with contempt.»*
1 Samuel 2:30(NRSV)

The first verses of the New Testament in the Gospel of Matthew open with a historical genealogy leading to the birth of Jesus. It is a passage that seems boring and is often skipped. However, students of the Bible have long noted how surprising the genealogy is. It contains people of all kinds of backgrounds. The stunning diversity portrayed in Matthew chapter 1 makes a cardinal point. History is His, Christ's, story! Romans states, "We know that all things work together for good for those who love God, who are called according to his purpose."[52] Put differently, history itself belongs to the creator God! The Lord is sovereign even here in the historical domain of existence.

The separation ripping the United Methodist Church and giving birth to the dawn of a new church, the Global Methodist Church, raises two significant questions that have informed our decision to leave the United Methodist Church and embrace the holy task of establishing a new Wesleyan witness. First, how are people to faithfully follow the Lord of history? Second, how does the separation taking place to align with the history of the Methodist (Wesleyan) movement?

The Quest for the "Right Side" of History

"It is important to get on the right side of history on this" the speaker declared. The words were uttered with forceful passion. The speaker was referring to the question of marriage for same-gender partners in the church and ordination for those in a committed same-gender relationship. The reference to the "right side of history" came in response to the churches' failure to stand up in the fight against slavery and the failure to abolish segregation. There was no doubt in his mind that those who opposed "full inclusion" (as he put it) were like those who had opposed integration in the 1960s. He was uncompromising as he presented marriage and ordination as "rights." Those who failed to support the speaker's understanding of "full inclusion" would come to regret their failure in the future just as those who fought against desegregation had come to a place of shame and regret for their failure to integrate.

The argument sounds reasonable. We all desire to be on the "right side of history." It is understandable to hope that as someone looks back on their life that they publicly supported the right and moral thing to do. Desegregation is such an issue. The problem with accessing the "right side of history" comes from the reality that such judgments are made in retrospect. Knowing what we know today, Winston Churchill's holding out against the evils of Nazi Germany looks heroic. Churchill was on the "right side of history." However, at the time well-meaning people and significant leaders like British Prime Minister Neville Chamberlain and Foreign Secretary Lord Halifax strongly supported a policy of peace (which in twenty-twenty hindsight is labeled appeasement). They thought they were on the right side of history. Clearly, they were not. Today Chamberlain and Halifax are examples of those who would have surrendered to evil in the false pursuit of an illusory peace.

The history of the Wesleyan movement in America exhibits the same struggle to discern correctly what is the right side of history. When Methodism first came to America church doctrine was clear. You could not be a slaveholder and be a Methodist. Tragically and reluctantly Francis Asbury and the early American Methodists compromised and allowed slaveholding in the Methodist Episcopal Church. As the abolitionist movement grew, the original Methodist movement experienced an early schism over slaveholding. Sixty years later the church was divided into the Methodist Episcopal Church (essentially North) and the Methodist Episcopal Church, South. History's judgment of the compromise on slavery and later reunion is clear about the "right side of history." It was not clear to many at the time.

There is a great danger in assuming that contemporary convictions and assertions automatically constitute the right side of history. Before World War II, it appeared that the future belonged to some version of authoritarianism and the rule of the "strong man." Thomas Ricks in *Churchill and Orwell: The Fight for Freedom* writes about how, by the 1930s, democracy was discredited in many circles. Authoritarian rule and rulers were everywhere considered to be the wave of the future. Many believed the complexity of modern life along with economic necessity dictated the rule of powerful leaders dominating ineffective democracies. With the benefit of hindsight, the contemporary assessment of the 1930s is now known to be tragically wrong. Likewise, for a period communism has been held to be the future of the world in a new and utopian society. It was, to many in elite circles, "the right side of history." Today we more properly view communism as a morally bankrupt failed system of economics and governance.

It is not an overstatement to assert that history is littered with examples of ideas, morality, and governance that looked to be the "right side of history" or the wave of the future only later to prove disastrous and be rightly tossed aside. However alluring, contemporary culture cannot be the only or even the primary judge of historical insight. God alone is Lord of history.

A careful caveat is in order. Christians must stay in a caring and thoughtful dialog with culture. It is important to understand the hurts, wants, and needs that swirl around us. We must communicate in a manner and style understandable to those we encounter in daily life. Loving compassion is simply a must, but loving compassion does not involve endorsing positions outside of a higher allegiance to the Lord. The earlier Christian aspiration to be "in but not of the world" must constantly serve as a guide. The crucial difference is that Christians are to operate under the rule of the Lord Jesus Christ. He alone is to be our master. We firmly reiterate, that however attractive and/or desirable a contemporary idea or position may be, it must be submitted to his lordship, to his ultimate rule and guidance. Jesus Christ is Lord of history. History is the ongoing story of God's unfolding creation as Father, Son, and Holy Spirit.

While it is important for us to understand the culture in which we live, discernment about what we should do as followers of Jesus must be faithful and obedient to the Lord of history. Fortunately, we are not the first people to wrestle with the dilemma of how to faithfully respond in history to God's unfolding purposes. Nor are we the first people to prefer our will over God's creative design. A biblical story is instructive.

In the Old Testament book of 1st Chronicles, chapter 12, Israel's first king, Saul, his son Jonathan, and his leading general, Abner, had just died and representatives of the tribes of Israel came to Hebron to name David King and pledge their allegiance to his leadership. The story begins with these words: "These are the numbers of the divisions of the armed troops who came to David in Hebron to turn the kingdom of Saul over to him [David], according to the word of the Lord."[53] They were coming to pledge their swords and lives to a new king who had been anointed by God upon the death of the old king Saul. The people were acting in obedience to God. One of the tribes listed were the sons of Issachar "who had an understanding of the times, to know what Israel ought to do, two hundred chiefs, and all their kindred under their command."[54]

Pause with us and investigate what was happening. The Bible says the sons of Issachar had an "understanding of the times, to know what Israel ought to do." Inquire as to what this means. Did they understand public relations and political alliances? Perhaps. Did they grasp the mood of the nation and the direction the political winds were blowing? Maybe—but understanding the signs of the times apart from spiritual discernment and obedience to God can quickly become political gamesmanship. Without a spiritual anchoring in the Lord of history, the signs of the times can easily descend into testing which way the wind blows or advocating for our predetermined preferences.

The sons of Issachar were engaged in radically different behavior than political or social posturing. They knew God was going to lead Israel through a new king. They understood they were in changing times yet remained consistent in their obedience to God. They had followed Saul while he lived—because God had chosen him. Even as David's popularity had increased, the sons of Issachar could not join David while Saul lived because God had chosen and anointed Saul. But, as soon as Saul, his son Jonathan and Abner were dead, the sons of Issachar could sense the changing times. They did not play the weathervane to popular opinion. They knew, spiritually discerned, that it was time for them to get behind David as their new king. In doing so they were doing what God told them, as they pledged their swords and lives to support David's leadership. The sons of Issachar were obedient to the God of Israel who had selected and anointed David as the new King. Their obedience to God's purposes and plans took precedence over their desires and ideas. They knew who the Lord of history was.

The lesson for us is clear and unmistakable. Obedience to God's will and way towers above our wants and wishes. Instead of wistfully trying to get on the right side of history, we are to be obedient to the Lord of history. The sons of Issachar offer contemporary Christians a model of behavior which merits emulation. As we struggle to discern "the right side of history," Holy Scripture offers profound guidance. As 1 Samuel admonishes us, "the Lord God declares ...those who honor me I will honor."[55]

Lest we think this is simply an Old Testament (Hebrew Bible) story that we can safely dismiss in the 21st century, we invite your consideration of a crucial incident that shaped the life of the early Christian movement. The first great Council of the Church is reported in Acts 15. A dispute arose over whether someone had to observe Jewish laws, specifically circumcision, first to become Christian.[56] As they debated the issue Peter stood up and gave a

Holy Spirit-inspired witness. "Why then are you now challenging God by placing a burden on the shoulders of these disciples that neither we nor our ancestors could bear? On the contrary, we believe that we and they are saved in the same way, by the grace of the Lord Jesus."[57]

Peter didn't seek popularity. His stance was not popular. Peter did not succumb to seeking the lowest common denominator of compromise. He was faithful and obedient to the Lord of history. In the great Jerusalem Council, those listening finally agreed.[58] Once again the words of 1 Samuel came true."

Living as we are in the third decade of the twenty-first century, the question before us is not, are we on the right side of history? The question before us is, are we faithful and obedient to the Lord? The sons of Issachar and the Apostle Peter model behavior we would do well to embrace. We want to be on the right side of history.

Christian Unity and the Wesleyan Movement

The second question which rightly intrudes at the dawn of a new church and a new or renewed expression of the Wesleyan way of being Christian is: How does the separation taking place to align with the history of the Methodist (Wesleyan) movement? In the debate over the separation taking place in the United Methodist Church and the dawn of the Global Methodist Church, there has arisen a position we will call "institutionalist." Pointing to the prayer of Jesus in John 17 that all may be one, some advocate institutional Christian unity as a more important value than doctrinal fidelity.

We wish to affirm that we too pray for and work towards Christian unity. Institutional coherence is important, but it is not the highest value. The Christian witness of faith over the entire history of the church universal (what we call the church with a big "C") has rejected valuing institutional unity and staying together at all costs, at the expense of faithfulness and allegiance to God as Father, Son, and Holy Spirit.

John 17 bears careful exegetical biblical study to understand its full impact. Jesus prays, "I ask not only on behalf of these but also on behalf of those who believe in me through their word, that they may all be one. As you, Father, are in me and I am in you, may they also be in us, so that the world may believe that you have sent me."[59] The Savior's prayer for unity is directed explicitly to the mission "so that the world may believe that you have sent me." The call and claim of true discipleship tower above institutional concerns (however valuable and important those institutional concerns may be).

Those who advocate unity at all costs should carefully consider it. A unity at all cost argument is, on the face of it, a rejection of the Protestant Reformation. If we are to accept institutional unity above all else, then United Methodists should be seeking to fold themselves into the Roman Catholic Church or the Eastern Orthodox Church (depending on which element one considers to have been right in the great schism of 1054 A.D.) If we believe in institutional Christian Unity as the highest value, then at a minimum United Methodists should resubmit themselves to the Church of England.[60]

The big "C" Church is the Church of Jesus Christ. It was born of the Spirit on Pentecost and comprises all the little "c" churches past, present, and future. The United Methodist Church as well as the dawning Global Methodist Church are only little "c" churches that are a very small part of the big "C" church. Little "c" churches exist to contribute to the larger mission all Christians share of making disciples of Jesus Christ and spreading the gospel throughout the earth.[61] The big "C" Church encompasses what we might consider differing views like Catholic and Protestant, clergy and laity, Baptist Presbyterian Methodist, etc., traditional and contemporary, priests and pastors, dunkers and sprinklers – and the various other categories that divide us. The big "C" Church reaches across time and space—and holds firm even as empires rise and fall. The big "C" Church is far bigger than the UMC or the GMC or any local church. We are called to be part of the big "C" Church.

In 18th Century England, the church had lost much of its heart and mission while the culture around it spun out of control. The church had gotten stuck in the way it did things. It was stale and ineffective. People living all around them were in desperate need of a Savior—but did not hear the message of the gospel because they were not even on the church's radar. In that context, God called two brothers, John and Charles Wesley—who had experienced a heart-warming, life-changing encounter with Jesus—to lead a movement that sparked a revival like the world had not seen since the time of the Apostles.

They were called Methodists because of the methods they used. They abandoned the systems and structures of churches of their day—and used new methods (particularly lay preaching and class meetings yoke to helping and healing ministry with the poor) to take the unchanging message of Jesus to the people. They preached outdoors connecting to people who were not welcome in church buildings and came out of the mines and mills. They put the message of the Gospel to the familiar melodies of the drinking songs of their day so the people would sing them. ("O for a Thousand Tongues to Sing" was set to a bar tune.) They met the needs of the poor so they would hear what was being shared. They brought deliverance to the addicted, advocated for women's, children's, and workers' rights, and fought against slavery. They offered plain truth to plain people, bringing hundreds of thousands of people in England and America to saving faith in Jesus Christ. Then the Methodists discipled them and taught them to obey everything Jesus had commanded. As Jesus changed their lives the Methodist movement changed the world.

John Wesley was once asked what he thought the future of the Methodists might look like. He answered, "I am not afraid that the people called Methodists should ever cease to exist either in Europe or America. But I am afraid, lest they should only exist as a dead sect, having the form of religion without the power. And this undoubtedly will be the case, unless they hold fast to both the doctrine, spirit, and discipline with which they first set out."[62]

Let those last words reverberate in your heart and mind. The message matters. Doctrinal teaching that faithfully holds Christ at the center of the Church (both big and little "C/c"), lives in disciplined obedience through holiness of heart and life matters! Sharing the gospel with others matters. What we believe impacts the way we live.

Throughout the history of the Christian faith, God has periodically raised new communities of faith (denominations as little "c" parts of the big "C" church universal). Methodism and the Wesleyan movement are no exception to God's creating determination to have a fresh and vibrant witness of the gospel offered to a bruised and battered world. This was not the first division in the Wesleyan Methodist movement in America. The African Methodist Episcopal Church (AME) was birthed as a response to the sin of slavery and segregation in 1787 (growing out of the Free African Society).[63] The O'Kelly schism (lead by James O'Kelly, a circuit rider and ardent abolitionist) lead to the split-off of what became known as the Christian Church over issues of the power of bishops and anti-slavery.[64] The Methodist Protestant Church left in 1828 again over issues of congregational church governance and the power (or alleged abuse of power) by bishops in appointment making. Kevin Watson brilliantly chronicled the expulsion of B. T. Roberts from Methodist Episcopal Church in 1860, which lead to the formation of the Free Methodist Church.[65] Significantly the 1910 General Conference of the Methodist Episcopal Church acknowledged that a mistake was made in expelling Rev. (later Bishop) B.T. Roberts and a formal apology was made to his son. The schism between the North and South branches of the Methodist Episcopal Church took place in 1844. The numerically large stream of American Methodists reunited the Methodist Episcopal Church (North), the Methodist Episcopal Church South, and the Methodist Protestant Church in 1939.

Many more examples could be added to this brief walk through the history of the Wesleyan and Methodist movement in America. Careful attention to the historical record will illuminate similar branches of Methodism around the world. What is taking place between the United Methodist Church and the Global Methodist Church is not an isolated "blip" in history but a par to a larger process of growth, struggle with doctrinal clarity, and the future of the Wesleyan witness to a larger world. The Global Methodist Church is steadfastly ecumenical in its orientation and seeks a wholesome Christian relationship with communities of faith including the United Methodist Church.

The first division among the Methodists over doctrinal differences occurred before the Movement even came to America. As a student and later professor at Oxford University, John Wesley helped form a small group of men who were serious about discipleship and growing their faith. They called it the Holy Club. Among its members were John Wesley, his younger brother, Charles, and a younger student named George Whitefield. John Wesley was the unquestioned thought and theological leader of the Methodist Revival. Charles Wesley was the great hymn-writer who put Methodist theological lyrics to the popular drinking tunes of their day. And George Whitefield was a young, but very effective preacher, who became the leader of what was referred to as the First Great Awakening.

As the Holy Club became more disciplined in the way they lived their life and held each other accountable, they began to be called "Methodists" because they were so methodical in their discipleship. They preached regularly for conversion and called Christians to live holy lives. They believed in free will and our need to choose to accept a relationship with God by placing faith in Jesus. They invited those who responded to their preaching to become "Methodist" in practice and meet in weekly small groups they called "class meetings." They held each other accountable to live their faith, give to the poor, feed the hungry, and began to address aspects of their culture they saw as counter to the Gospel—like unjust child labor, drunkenness, and slavery. With their emphasis on personal and social holiness. Methodists began to change their world.

When John and Charles Wesley went on their failed missionary journey to America in 1735, they left the Methodist Movement in the hands of George Whitefield. But by the time the Wesleys returned from America, George Whitefield had become a Calvinist. Which, in oversimplified terms, is a Protestant theology that believes in a supernatural power that controls human destiny. This may not seem like a big deal to you, but to John Wesley, this was a huge deal.

To put it mildly, Wesley and Whitefield had a sharp disagreement. At first, it was private, but eventually, their theological disagreement became public. Both Wesley and Whitefield were immensely popular. Both preached their messages with conviction and power, engaged in open public debates, and wrote and printed open letters to each other attacking the other's views in the London papers.

Wesley emphasized the Arminian understanding of free will—the God-given capacity for us to choose to respond to the grace of God by faith. In other words, we get to choose to respond to grace. Whitefield embraced a Calvinist understanding of predestination—the belief that God predestines or chooses who will respond to grace and who will not—meaning God chooses who goes to heaven and who goes to hell. Wesley and Whitefield parted ways as partners in ministry. They never questioned each other's faith in Jesus, but they did question each other's beliefs and practices.

This open conflict between the two greatest revival preachers of their day began to damage their witnesses and weaken their message. It's in this context Wesley wrote his famous sermon "A Catholic Spirit." It's the 39th of his 44 Standard Sermons. Wesley first published this sermon in 1755 amid his ongoing disagreement with George Whitefield—to teach Christians how to treat each other when we have differences of opinion.

In this sermon, Wesley made it clear: opinions matter but are not the most important. Even though we have different opinions, it doesn't mean we can't love each other. Some have interpreted this to mean differences of opinion should never divide us by quoting from the sermon: "Though we can't think alike, may we not love alike?"[66] This is one of the most misquoted statements of Wesley. It's the go-to quote for Methodists who argue that Wesley wasn't interested in sound doctrine just having a good heart. Nothing could be further from the truth. We're convinced most people who use this quote have not read much of John Wesley, much less this sermon. The entire context of the misquoted Wesley says: "But although a difference in opinions or modes of worship may prevent an entire external union, yet need it to prevent our union in affection? Though we can't think alike, may we not love alike? May we not be of one heart, though we are not of one opinion? Without all doubt, we may. Herein all the children of

God may unite, notwithstanding these smaller differences. These remaining as they are, they may forward one another in love and good works."[67] This context reveals this sermon isn't a call to stay together at all costs, but it does have a lot to say about how we treat each other in our disagreements. Wesley tried to teach us how to engage in conflict and differences of opinion with love—a generous affection for each other.

So, what does this catholic spirit—this generous affection—look like? First, let's begin by clarifying what Wesley said a catholic spirit is not. A catholic spirit is not indifferent to other beliefs, practices, or denominations. A Christian should believe and practice what they believe is most faithful to Christ and belong to a little "c" church that affirms those beliefs and practices. Wesley wasn't asking us to look the other way about differences in essential beliefs items. Doctrine matters. We're not being asked to go along to get along. Wesley called this "the spawn of hell, not the offspring of heaven; an irreconcilable enemy, not a friend, to a catholic spirit."[68]

Wesley said: "Observe this, you who know not what spirit ye are of, who call yourselves men of a catholic spirit only because you are of a muddy understanding; because your mind is all in a mist; because you have no settled, consistent principles, but are for jumbling all opinions together. Be convinced that you have quite missed your way: you know not where you are. You think you are got into the very spirit of Christ when in truth you are nearer the spirit of antichrist. God first and learn the first elements of the gospel of Christ, and then shall you learn to be of a truly catholic spirit."[69]

Loving one another isn't a call to be a doormat. Loving one another doesn't put feeling above sound doctrine, but it does determine the way we express our disagreements. We're called to love our neighbors as ourselves—even if they have a different opinion. To love our enemy and pray for those who persecute us—even in the thick of the fight. A catholic spirit enables us to say: "If your heart is like my heart, give me your hand"[70] with integrity. Wesley never intended for us to set aside major differences and just go along to get along. We can't all think alike (beliefs). We can't all walk alike (practices). But we can all respect each other's opinions.

We believe the Lord of History is calling us to set ourselves apart from the UMC in matters of doctrine and practice. We wish we could find a way to bless and send our respective understandings of what it means to be a little "c" church into our respective futures, but it appears our polity is making this more and more difficult. Yet, even in the face of this time of conflict and uncertainty, we call for us all to embody the best of a catholic spirit and offer generous affection to one another. We believe the Lord of History demands it.

Let these words of Wesley be our guide: "But while he is steadily fixed in his religious principles in what he believes to be the truth as it is in Jesus; while he firmly adheres to that worship of God which he judges to be most acceptable in his sight; and while he is united by the most tender and close ties to one particular congregation, his heart is enlarged toward all mankind, those he knows and those he does not; he embraces with strong and cordial affection both neighbours and strangers, friends and enemies. This is catholic or universal love. And he that has this is of a catholic spirit. For love alone gives the title to this character: catholic love is a catholic spirit."[71]

SECTION II

A RENEWED WESLEYAN MOVEMENT OF FAITH IN THE GLOBAL METHODIST CHURCH

CHAPTER 5:
THE CHALLENGE BEFORE US

Now I want you to understand, brothers and sisters, the good news that I proclaimed to you, which you in turn received, in which also you stand, through which also you are being saved, if you hold firmly to the message that I proclaimed to you—unless you have come to believe in vain. For I handed on to you as of first importance what I in turn had received: that Christ died for our sins in accordance with the scripture and that he was buried and that he was raised on the third day in accordance with the scriptures.
1 Corinthians 15:1-4(NRSV)

The words strike at the heart of the gospel. "I want you to understand!"[72] writes the Apostle Paul. The Apostle reaches toward the conclusion of his first letter to the troubled church in Corinth. He does not outline how to be a better institutional church. He does not coddle them. Paul metaphorically leans forward with deepened emphasis. Through this gospel message (and none other!) we "are being saved." The emphasis redounds with the plea that the Corinthians must hold to this gospel truth "firmly" and then a warning "unless you have come to believe in vain." What he has to share is of "first importance!"

The challenge before us is to return to the essence of the gospel message. We are called to do so in a time when Christianity is no longer the dominant belief or faith of most people in our contemporary culture. We're being challenged again to reconvert the continent and the world in the face of massive cultural indifference.

We invite the reader to overhear a very different conversation. The conversation took place on a casual vacation Saturday afternoon in the San Francisco area almost two decades ago. As we sat in the backyard with my brother and sister-in-law, my wife and I (Bishop Lowry) inquired about what local churches were nearby where we could worship God the next day. Scott and Sharon do not belong to any local church and give no evidence of any deep religious convictions. With charity and without condemnation, they are not Christian. But Jolynn and I thought they knew the area and so we inquired.

The two of them fumbled around trying to think of the nearest United Methodist Church. After a while, they decided there might be one on a certain street a couple of miles away. They weren't sure. I checked online and found the worship times. We invited them to go with us. Scott's answer was an intriguing one. He said, "Why? Why bother?" He said, "If I go, they're going to tell me to be a nice person, to help others, and out here they're going to advocate something that sort of looks like the liberal wing of the Democratic Party. Well," he continued, "I think I am a nice person. (For the record, I agree. He's a good person and a moral man.) And I've tried being a liberal Democrat. I don't think it works. I've tried," he said, "being a conservative Republican. I don't think that much works either. He paused to reflect adding something like this: "I appreciate the invitation, but why would we want to bother going to church? Even more, why would we want to bother being Christian?"

The Battle with Moralistic Therapeutic Deism

We need to separate the Christian faith from American culture. We've always been at our best and most vibrant when we're distinctive, but from time to time, the people of God lose our vibrancy because we try too much to be like the people around us. When the culture begins to infiltrate, change, or obliterate what it means to live as God's people—we cease to be the people God calls us to be.

George Barna's Faith to Action research has discovered the percentage of Americans who identify as having no religious affiliation has risen from 25 to 50% between 2019 and 2021. Of the remaining 50% who do claim a religious affiliation, not all identify as Christian, and those who do identify as Christian often don't profess historic Christianity or hold a distinctively Biblical worldview.

Out of his February 2021 survey, Barna concluded that MTD—Moralistic Therapeutic Deism—is the most popular worldview in the United States today. Barna said, "Christianity in this nation is rotting from the inside out. MTD is essentially what I would call fake Christianity. Because it has some Christian elements in it, but it's not really biblical and it's not really Christian."[73] And what exactly is MTD? Barna answers: "The MORALISTIC perspective is we're here to be good people and to try to do good."[74] How many of us know good folks who are simply trying to be good people?

"The THERAPEUTIC aspect is everything is supposed to be geared to making me feel good about myself—ultimately to make me happy."[75] We're surrounded by folks doing whatever they want to feel good about themselves and be happy.

"DEISM is the idea that God—like a cosmic clockmaker—created the world and set it in motion—but has no direct involvement in it. Basically, according to MTD, there's a distant, but impersonal God who just wants everyone to be nice, and the purpose of life is to be happy. Cultural "Christians" who've adopted this philosophy often elevate personal definitions of right and wrong above any objective standard of truth—like the Bible."[76] In this scenario, the individual is the sole determiner of all that is good and true. We feel better already!

A comparison between the "faith that was once and for all handed on to all the saints"[77] and Moralistic Therapeutic Deism demonstrates a massive disconnect. MTD is no longer the faith of the Apostles. MTD is directly opposite of historic, orthodox Christianity which teaches us we live in a fallen creation that bears the mark of sin—especially in us. It's impossible for us to ultimately be good and do good without addressing the problem of our sin. While we desire to be good and do good, holiness of heart and life cannot be achieved apart from the grace of God. While we may need therapy to help us move forward toward happiness, our faith teaches us the goal is not just happiness, but also transformation—to be changed from who and what we are dead in our sin—to becoming the person God created and redeemed us to be. It is well to recall the marvelous summary of God's redemptive action in Jesus Christ as Savior and Lord as expressed by bishops Irenaeus and Athanasius, two of the theological giants of early Christianity, who said: "He [Jesus] became like us that we might become like him."[78]

The God of the Bible is so much more than a detached, dispassionate, cosmic clockmaker who created the world, set it in motion, and has no interest or involvement in our lives like Deism teaches. We believe in an incarnational God who loved us so much He became one of us—that's what that fancy word incarnational means, God became flesh in Jesus, lived a perfect life, and died a sacrificial death to save anyone who believes in Him.

The "faith" embraced by most Americans today is not the "singular" faith proclaimed by John Wesley who said, "You must be singular or be damned!"[79] Nor is it the confident faith of the Apostle Paul who said, "that Christ died for our sins in accordance with the scriptures and that he was buried and that he was raised on the third day in accordance with the Scriptures."[80] It's also not what we declare in the Apostle's Creed: "I believe in God the Father Almighty, Creator of heaven and earth and in Jesus Christ, His only Son, our Lord." No. Cultural Christianity's faith isn't even anchored in the bold exclusivity of Jesus himself, who said, "I am the way, the truth, and the life. No one comes to the Father but through me!"[81]

Cultural Christianity isn't anything this stable—this historical—this enduring—this deep—or this true. It's a combination of "I'm OK, you're OK," "Don't worry, be happy!", "You be you," "You do you," and feel-good religion as we celebrate and legitimize all that ails us. Moralistic Therapeutic Deism manipulates and distorts the God of the Bible to make the Lord bless all the brokenness and vanities of the modern world.

When Christianity starts to be more American (or any other nation) than it is Christian—or when the culture infiltrates, changes, or obliterates what it means to be distinctively Christian—it's time to take a step back and remember exactly what Jesus came to do. Perceptively Professor George Hunter reminds us as students that early Christianity grew in part because it refused to be syncretic.[82]

The Challenge Before Us

Over the years the question of my brother and his wife has grown. "Why would we want to bother going to church? Even more, why would we want to bother being Christian?" They are before us in stark terms. Many, indeed millions, intuitively and readily grasp the need for a spiritual and moral dimension to their lives. Dwight Eisenhower's assertion resonates across cultural lines today more so than when he first uttered the words. "Our form of government makes no sense unless it is founded in a deeply felt religious belief, and I don't care what it is."[83] Spirituality is not debated. The challenge is what kind of spirituality. What kind of spiritual convictions, dare we say faith, should we hold? Even more concretely, the challenge before Christians must be faced without flinching. *Why bother being Christian?*

Why bother, indeed? Cannot life be good, full, and satisfying without any real connection with God? Further, it is possible to be spiritual without being religious? (I have no idea what "spiritual but not religious" means and/or looks like. We assert that the very concept of SBNR – spiritual but not religious – is philosophical nonsense; literally, it makes no sense.) The answer is no. You can't be "spiritual" but not religious. Spirituality implies some form of religion as the philosophical foundation of that spirituality, however inchoate and loosely organized it might be. The more sophisticated question is what or how you are religious – Christian, Buddhist, Muslim, Hindu, or your concoction (a religious version of the so-called "Singapore Sling" that my (Bishop Lowry) college buddies insisted I drink when I turned 21; the "Singapore

Sling" was a concoction of 7 or 8 different types of alcohol mixed and designed to produce an alcohol high). The "why" question attaches itself to us and our time like a piece of Velcro that will not be shaken off. It drives us back to reclaiming the heart of the Christian faith.

This is not a new question. What is new is the way "church" is divorced from religious experience and the intensity with which Christians are being challenged by this question. Another version of the challenge of 'why bother?' came from a lay leader in the Central Texas Conference. He challenged a group of clergy who focused the gospel narrowly on various deeds of service and acts of social justice. His challenge was phrased this way. "Why can't I just volunteer and work on a Habitat House? Why do I need to be part of the church?"

What should disturb us greatly is how poorly we are equipped to face the challenge of why. It is worth pausing to note carefully that the challenge which originates in the question 'why to bother to be a part of a church or worship?' quickly connects to the deeper challenge 'why bother to be a Christian at all?' The heart of the issue is profoundly theological and deeply biblical.

It has been said that the evangelical or conservative wing of the Christian movement in America is the Republican Party at prayer. To which one can easily add that the liberal or progressive wing of the Christian movement in America is the Democrat Party gathered around a Habitat House. Despite the obvious distortion of the Christian movement across the American spectrum, both tongue-in-check statements carry a painful grain of truth. Furthermore, despite a richly biblical and theological tradition, the very catch phrase "spiritual but not religious" betrays the need for a clear and convincing answer to the challenge of why.

Contrast the mainline churches' poverty in providing an answer to the challenge of why with an urban legend about John Wimber, the founder of the Vineyard Church movement. The legend goes something like this.

Wimber's conversion to Christianity by his admission came from a life in the counterculture of the 1960s and early 1970s. Confessing Christ as both Lord and Savior, he repented (that is literally "changed his heart and life"). Turning his life over to Christ as Lord in full allegiance, he began attending a local church. After coming and sharing in worship for three or four Sundays, he stopped an usher at the door. Legend has it he asked the guy, "When do we do the stuff?" Puzzled the kindly usher replied, "What stuff do you mean?" As the story goes, John Wimber shot back, "You know, the healing, casting out demons and experiencing the Holy Spirit." Catching on to the credulous expression of the befuddled usher Wimber is reported to have continued, "I gave up sex and drugs for this! It better be good! When do we get to get into the Spirit?"

Wimber's overwhelming transformational conversion to the Christian faith and the person and work of Christ contrasts sharply with vague politeness that calls on us to be nice and join the preferred political party (whatever that is!). The decline of an identifiable "Christian" difference speaks volumes to a fear-soaked, morally adrift, spiritually and physically hungry world.

The Struggle to Reclaim the Christian Truth

Perhaps more telling than all the other signs of the moral and philosophical wilderness (the disestablishment of the church and Christian faith in society, cultural indifference to deeper issues of faith especially in younger generations, and dwindling church membership, -- combined with general ignorance of foundational Christian beliefs and ethical tenants) the Christian church finds itself in is the theological wilderness we have entered. Basic presuppositions are under dispute. Popular culture even rejects the very notion of truth with a capital "T" with bizarre phrases like "alternative facts." Much of the so-called western culture regards religious truth as a matter of personal preference.

Jesus offers great insight in his foundational teaching and preaching as recorded in the Sermon on the Mount. "Everybody who hears these words of mine and puts them into practice is like a wise builder who built a house on bedrock. The rain fell, the floods came, and the wind blew and beat against that house. It didn't fall because it was firmly set on bedrock. But everybody who hears these words of mine and doesn't put them into practice will be like a fool who built a house on sand. The rain fell, the floods came, and the wind blew and beat against that house. It fell and was completely destroyed."[84] The loss of difference reflects our failure to build our philosophical and theological house on the bedrock of Christ. Once again C. S. Lewis is prophetic. "A world of nice people, content in their own niceness, looking no further, turned away from God, would be just as desperately in need of salvation as a miserable world and might even be more difficult to save."[85]

There is no clear trumpet that sounds the call of orthodoxy for the old mainline denominations. To paraphrase from I Samuel, the word of the Lord is rare in these days; visions are not widespread.[86] The philosophical decline of our faith foundation highlights the deeply embedded sense of social and moral relativism.

One of the great Christian leaders in the 20th century was the missionary, bishop, evangelist, and theologian Lesslie Newbigin. He made his mark in courageous and pioneering work spreading the gospel and speaking out for justice in India. Two decades ago, in *Foolishness to the Greeks: The Gospel and Western Culture*, Newbigin wrote as a cultural analysis that "The result is not, as we once imagined, a secular society. It is a pagan society, and its paganism, having been born out of the rejection of Christianity, is far more resistant to the gospel than the pre-Christian paganism with which cross-Christian missions have been familiar."[87]

Late in life, this great Christian leader returned home to his native Britain. Professor William Abraham reports: "A moving point of entry into Newbigin's thinking about the prospects for the church in the West can be found in the penultimate chapter of his memoirs. In 1979, Newbigin found himself presiding over the Birmingham District Council of the United Reformed Church. In the course of the meeting, they had to face the possibility of closing an old church outside Winson Green prison. Newbigin could not contemplate such a decision. In the end, he became the pastor on a part-time basis.

'On 2 January I was duly installed and since then I have been struggling to fulfill the obligations of this ministry. It is much harder than anything I met in India. There is a cold contempt for the gospel which is harder to face than opposition. As I visit the Asian homes in the district, most of them Sikhs or Hindus, I find a welcome which is often denied on the doorsteps of the natives. I have been forced to recognize that the most difficult missionary frontier in the contemporary world is the one of which the Churches have been—on the whole—so little conscious, the frontier that divides the world of biblical faith from the world whose values and beliefs are ceaselessly fed into every home on the television screen. Like others I have been accustomed, especially in the 1960s, to speak of England as a secular society. I have now come to realize that I was the easy victim of an illusion from which my reading of the Gospels should have saved me. No room remains empty for long. If God is driven out, the gods come trooping in. *England is a pagan society and the development of a truly missionary encounter with this very tough form of paganism is the greatest intellectual and practical task facing the church.'"88*

To our great consternation, the false gods' have rushed in. Polytheism has re-emerged in a hidden guise. There are the standard culprits of materialism, hedonism, racism, power, greed, and the like. In a profound sense, they are always present. What is different in these times is the assertion that basic standards of judgment largely no longer apply. The very claim to "Truth" as standing above and in some sense beyond our human pretensions and cultural claims is in dispute. Pilate's age-old question "What is truth?"89 is being asked again in dramatically new ways.

I (Bishop Lowry) recall as a student taking a required course in Methodist Doctrine and Polity taught by the great twentieth-century theologian Albert C. Outler at Perkins School of Theology, Southern Methodist University. Carefully Professor Outler laid out the notion that the fence line for Methodist doctrine was wide, very wide but that there was a fence line. More recently Professor Justo Gonzales in introducing a popular new theology class for the United Methodist Church called *Christian Believer* employed baseball imagery to describe core theological concepts. He stated that doctrinal truth exists between the foul lines. Like Outler, Gonzales is willing to allow for a generously wide field. There is plenty of room between right field and left field. However, he insists that the foul lines do exist. In the theological wilderness of today's Methodism, the very notion of foul lines is up for grabs.

The famous Methodist quadrilateral (Scripture, tradition, reason, and experience) offered as a theological method threatens to replace the content of doctrine. "It is fascinating that after 1968 the *Doctrines and Discipline* became merely the *Book of Discipline*. It is difficult to imagine a more telling symbol of the deep shift which took place amount United Methodists."[90] Furthermore, the quadrilateral is often reduced to a bilateral or simply the citation of one point of the quadrilateral to support a pre-determined position. Quite famously John Wesley said, "But as to all opinions which do not strike at the root of Christianity, we think and let think."[91] Such a grand theological stance as John Wesley's presumes that there are in fact roots. Those who quote Wesley's openness with such ease fail to properly understand the context of Wesley's address. He could assume a mother church steeped in the ethos, ethics, and theology of Christendom.

Today we can make no such assumption. Indeed, another Wesley quote, a plea really, is more apropos. "I am sick of opinions. I am weary to bear them. My soul loathes this frothy food. Give me solid and substantial religion. Give me a humble, gentle lover of God and man."[92]

Not only has the mainline become the sideline, the established become the disestablished, but we have in large part lost even the basic Christian memory and reflexes that used to inform and guide us. We have left the comfortableness of Egypt and now are journeying in the wilderness of a new spiritual landscape.

In this barren theological and spiritual landscape, the renewed Methodism being birthed through the dawn of the Global Methodist Church dares to plant the flag of the Christian faith.

CHAPTER 6:
RECLAIMING THE HEART OF THE CHRISTIAN FAITH

We proclaim Christ crucified, a stumbling block to Jews and foolishness to Gentiles, but to those who are the called, both Jews and Greeks, Christ the power of God and the wisdom of God.
1 Corinthians 1:23-24 (NRSV)

The wacky *Back to the Future* movie trilogy popularized by Michael J. Fox and Christopher Lloyd points the way to a reclaiming of the original Methodist movement. The future of a renewed Methodism in the dawn of a new Global Methodist Church will live through a biblical, spiritual, and theological reclaiming of the heart of the Christian faith. The future to which we must go back will exhibit the biblical narrative of being in the world but not of it.

Over thirty-two years ago, Stanley Hauerwas and William Willimon reminded an entire generation of United Methodists that they were to be "resident aliens." They opened their best-selling work by directing attention to the Moffatt translation of Philippians 3:20. "We are a colony of heaven."[93] A colony, they pointed out, is "an island of one culture in the middle of another."[94] This theme of Christ and culture will dominate the shaping of the Global Methodist Church. This will be especially true in America as the country even more fully descends into a post-Christendom nation.

The North American (and much of the "industrial" world's) courtship of hedonistic materialism inescapably clashes with a deep Christian faith. Together we must learn again the lessons gained by early Christians living as a persecuted minority in Greco-Roman culture. The original Methodist movement in England was also a counter-cultural movement. We have much to learn and re-learn from those first Methodists. By going back to our future, we will gain valuable insights into the way of faith. Nowhere will this be truer than in the local church. (A brief but important side note. There are large parts of today's world where Christianity is a minority and sometimes persecuted faith. We have much to learn as well from our brothers and sisters in the faith outside of North America.)

In a prescient little book well worth our time and attention, Professor Scott Kisker of United Theological Seminary reminds us that we have a foundational choice to make. We can be "mainline" or "Methodist."[95] He writes:

> "The question for United Methodist today [and I would emphatically add for the dawning Global Methodist Church] is, 'Where do we go from here? The answer to that question depends on whether our church will locate its identity in its relationship to the culture or in its origins as a movement of the Holy Spirit in history. To many of us, the answer is clear: the purpose ... should be to embody the distinctive Wesleyan tradition of the apostolic and universal Christian faith. . . . Real Methodism declined because we replaced those peculiarities that made us Methodist with a bland, acceptable, almost civil religion, barely distinguishable from other traditions also now known as 'mainline.'"[96]

We must go back to a future of faithfulness. The early Christian church/movement and the Methodist revival of the 18th century will serve as guides.

The Foundational Framework of the Local Church

The foundational framework of the local church in the Next Methodism will have at a minimum four essential pillars. Vibrant faithful local congregations will exhibit qualities of being:

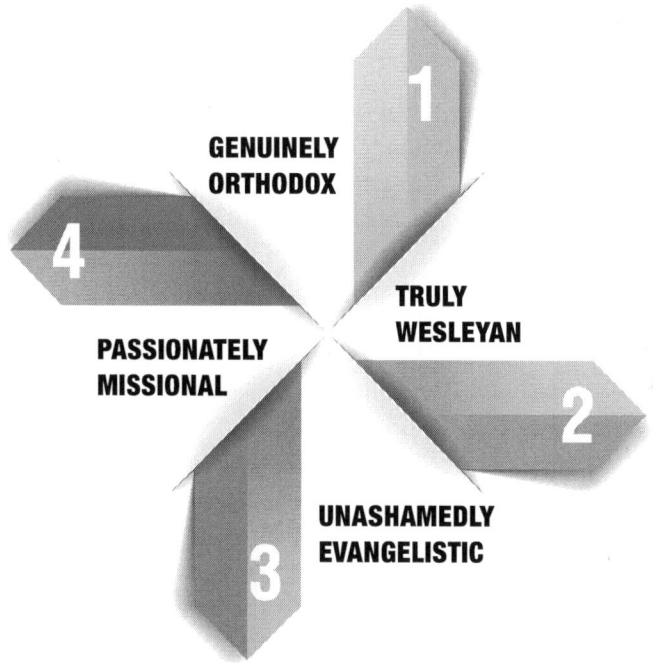

Genuinely orthodox will involve a relearning and re-commitment to the historic theological core of the Christian faith. This begins with an understanding of Holy Scripture as "the primary source and criterion for Christian doctrine"[97] and embraces the historic affirmations of Christian tradition. While open to honest inquiry, a genuine orthodoxy is anchored in the historic witness of Scripture, the Apostles and Nicaean creeds, the early ecumenical councils, and "Articles of Religion" as passed on from John Wesley. A renewed Methodist movement in the dawn of a new Global Methodist Church at the local church level must resist being tossed about by the winds of doctrinal speculation and theological fads. It is important to note that such conviction necessitates that theological education, pastoral training, and spiritual formation in leadership (both lay and clergy) development be clear and explicit in sharing the historically orthodox Christian faith.

While remaining deeply anchored in classical Christian orthodoxy, the renewed Methodism we envision in the dawn of a new Global Methodist Church will also remain open to new insight and theological development. The Christian adage of being "in but not of" the world again serves as a template for an intellectual stance that is simultaneously orthodox and open. A part of the genius of the early Methodist revival was its ability to stay culturally connected without succumbing to the dictates of culture. This will be a critical task for the Global Methodist Church at the local church level. It will require a nimbleness of both thought and practice that is proactive and not obsessively reactive while simultaneously being clear about what is believed and taught (as well as what is not believed and not taught!).

Genuinely orthodox means being unafraid of wrestling with great truths in the modern context while remaining anchored to the historic Christian faith. Great churches deal with great issues. Being genuinely orthodox is a launching pad, not a defensive fortification. It is a way of moving forward not a manner of retrenching. A genuine orthodoxy serves as a guide for engaging popular culture while maintaining clear and coherent boundaries. It is not a censoring tool for limiting discussion but rather a foundational starting point for theological inquiry. The words of Jesus in Matthew 7 illuminate the function of being genuinely orthodox. "Everyone then who hears these words of mine and acts on them will be like a wise man who built his house on the rock. The rain fell, the floods came, and the winds blew and beat on that house, but it did not fall, because it had been founded on the rock. And everyone who hears these words of mine and does not act on them will be like a foolish man who built his house on sand. The rain fell, and the floods came, and the winds blew and beat against that house, and it fell—and great was its fall!"[98]

Truly Wesleyan involves unambiguous and yet graciously ecumenical teaching and sharing of the Wesleyan understanding of the Christian faith. Key Wesleyan distinctives will be taught, embraced, and lived out in practice.[99]

The Wesleyan distinctives held at a minimum are a "high Christology" with Jesus as Lord, fully human and fully divine; sin as a malignant disease; the fullness of salvation in prevenient, justifying, and sanctifying grace; the lived implementation of sanctification as "holiness of heart and life;" and life as a disciplined follower (i.e., disciple). This pillar of a renewed Methodism in the local church offers a way of being a Christian; a "Method." Albert Cook Outler went so far as to assert that Wesley's originality came in this distinctive understanding of "faith alone and holy living held together."[100] "John Wesley believed and taught an explicit doctrine of holiness as the goal and crown of the Christian life."[101]

Wesley's understanding of the fulness of salvation serves as a crucial beginning point. One clear sign of a return to vibrant spiritual health in local churches of the Global Methodist Church will be a renewed embrace of a high Christology and a doctrine of salvation. Pastoral teaching will offer Wesley and the Wesleyan distinctives without apology. "What faith is it then through which we are saved?... it is faith in Christ – Christ, and God through Christ, are the proper object of it." ... it is not barely a speculative, rational, thing, a cold, lifeless assent, a train of ideas in the head."[102] Wesley goes on to say in his famous sermon "Salvation by Faith" that this is a "present salvation."[103] Professor Kevin Watson's one-sentence summary compactly offers the essence of Wesley's insistence on the fullness of salvation. "Salvation by faith is trust and confidence in the work of Jesus Christ to forgive us, reconcile us to God, and enable our growth in righteousness and true holiness."[104]

What is at stake in teaching the "Wesleyan Way" is a rejection of latent predestination and an insistence on the "order of salvation" moving through prevenient, justifying, and sanctifying grace. There is more, much more to be said here. For now, let the emphasis be lodged in the theological (belief) stress for the local church of a renewed Methodism in a doctrinal grounding combining both classical orthodoxy and the Wesleyan distinctives yoked to a lived Christian faith that demonstrates holiness of heart and life. As stated before, this will not come easy. It will surely involve a deep cultural change within most local churches. It will not be a quick process but rather one involving decades. The tectonic plates of domesticated Methodism will grind hard against the reborn vibrancy of a new Methodist movement. Painfully, a fair number of those individuals and churches who simply think they are choosing the conservative side in cultural war by joining the GMC will not survive the move to a renewed Methodism.

The very heart of being truly Wesleyan will be the recovery of an active, practiced doctrine of sanctification. We have a rich theological and missional heritage that continues to provide a unique, flexible, and strong framework for building the kinds of churches that are best suited to bring health, healing, and home to a battered and bruised world. Our insistence is that justification and sanctification go together – a personal relationship with Christ as Lord and Savior inseparably twined with a deep social justice, love, and mercy for all of God's children, creatures, and creation itself. The original vision of Methodism still towers above the landscape – "to reform the nation and, in particular, the Church, and spread scriptural holiness across the land."[105]

Being **Unashamedly evangelistic** is both a necessity for institutional survival and a missional imperative given by the risen Christ. If ever there is a word that has gone from Jerusalem to Jericho and fallen among thieves, it is the word evangelism. If ever there is a ministry that has been neglected in most local churches, it is the ministry of evangelism. We have lived so long with a historical reliance on Christendom that true evangelism through offering Christ has faded from active memory. It is accurately asserted that for generations most clergies were trained to change people's institutional commitment but not their essential life orientation and allegiance. Evangelism is about "tactics for sharing the good news." With Apostle Paul, a renewed Methodism will live in witness, faith sharing, and active apologetics. "I pray that the sharing of your faith may become effective when you perceive all the good that we may do for Christ."[106]

Unashamedly evangelistic means we will engage in the making of disciples of Jesus Christ in answer to the great commission given by the risen Christ without apology or pause. Sharing the good news (gospel) of salvation in and through Christ will once again be the essence of who we are in both thought and action.

Ed Stetzer in a *Christianity Today* 2015 article planted a flag in the ground on the meaning and practice of evangelism. "Evangelism," he wrote, "is not even outreach. Outreach can lead to evangelism, but you can have outreach all day and never announce the good news of the gospel of Jesus Christ. Evangelism is when people are challenged directly with the gospel and invited to respond. Many people may stumble at that point, but we always want people to hear and respond to the good news of the Gospel."[107]

An Anglican definition of evangelism attributed to Archbishop William Temple is still pertinent. "To evangelize is to so present Christ Jesus in the power of the Holy Spirit that men [people] shall come to put their trust in God through Him, to accept Him as their Savior, and serve Him as their King in the fellowship of His church."[108]

This is foreign territory to most of the current United Methodist Church in the early 21ˢᵗ century America and will be foreign to many moving into the Global Methodist Church. A Cabinet colleague of mine (Bishop Lowry) when I served as an episcopal leader in the Central Texas Conference of the UMC commented, "most pastors want to go to a larger church which somebody else grew." Reclaiming the evangelistic task is a profoundly "back to the future" activity. For many in current "mainline" Methodism, there is little need to evangelize. Indeed, one currently fashionable school of thought reduces evangelism to hospitality (radical or otherwise). However well intended, such an understanding leeches evangelism of its essential impetus and deeper theological content. A vague theological commitment to universal salvation obviates the need to be engaged in offering Christ. The theological incoherence of modern syncretistic theism clothed in Christian garb and slathered with cheap grace serves as an excuse to avoid evangelistic faith sharing.

The very nature of being unapologetically evangelistic will link a genuinely orthodox understanding of salvation through Christ alone with the rediscovery of faith sharing and explicit witnessing. Offering Christ to those who do not know him and/or follow him must once again become a core practice of the Christian faith. Bob Dylan's old album *Slow Train Coming* (in his Christian phase) has a classic song called: " Gotta serve somebody."[109] The reality of sin and the necessity of salvation demand a reclaiming of the evangelistic task by those who seek to be faithful Christ followers.[110]

The Apostle to the Gentiles speaks to us and our age. "When I came to you, brothers and sisters, I did not come proclaiming the mystery of God to you in lofty words or wisdom. For I decided to know nothing among you except Jesus Christ, and him crucified."[111] The great commission has not been repealed. "Go therefore and make disciples of all nations, baptizing them in the name of the Father and of the Son and of the Holy Spirit, and teaching them to obey everything that I have commanded you."[112]

Often misquoted, D. T. Niles's famous definition of evangelism makes the explicit connection between evangelism and confessing Christ. "EVANGELISM is witness. It is one beggar telling another beggar where to get food. . . . The Christian stands alongside the non-Christian and points to the Gospel, the holy action of God. It is not his knowledge of God that he shares, it is to God Himself that he points. The Christian Gospel is the Word become flesh."[113]

Out of the theological linkage of a recovered doctrine of soteriology with the practice of offering Christ to others will come a renewed vibrancy and deepening faithfulness in the local church. A renewed Methodism in the Global Methodist Church will, without apology, be in the business of helping churches grow in ways that are both faithful and fruitful. Near the close of the second chapter of the Acts of the Apostles, we learn that "those who welcomed his message were baptized, and that day about three thousand persons were added."[114] A few short verses later, the biblical record is even more specific. "And day by day the Lord added to their number those who were being saved."[115] Evangelistic church growth in numbers and discipleship is a future to be embraced.

Not long ago, twelve boys and their football (soccer) coach were trapped in a cave in Thailand that threatened to become a watery grave. A multi-national risky daring rescue was undertaken to find them and lead them to safety. Various rescue plans were attempted including pumping water outside the cave. Other possible options of waiting out the monsoons through a massive resupply effort were considered. Drilling down to the boys (trapped 2.5

miles from the cave entrance) was contemplated. Ultimately, rescue divers lead them to safety through the narrow dangerous passages. Two divers lost their lives in the effort. Reports indicated that "The rescue effort involved over 10,000 people including more than 100 divers, scores of rescue workers, representatives from about 100 governmental agencies, 900 police officers, and 2,000 soldiers; and it required ten police helicopters, seven ambulances, more than 700 diving cylinders, and the pumping of more than a billion litres of water from the caves."[116]

A passionately evangelistic church will operate like the rescue workers on the outside. Local churches of a renewed Methodism will not react like victims of societal change huddling together for warmth as death overtakes them. The early Christian community risked its own life in unapologetic evangelism through heroic attempts to reach those in the collapsing Roman Empire. Instead of staying cocooned for safety during times of epidemics, Christians reach out with medical help while sharing the gospel of Christ. Going "back to the future," a renewed Methodism will courageously reach out to those who do not know Christ.

This third pillar leads naturally to a strengthening of the fourth pillar.

Passionately missional, a renewed Methodism in the local church will be committed and actively engaged in combating injustice and oppression. At its most basic, this is living out the great commandment to love God and love our neighbor as we love ourselves.[117] Rick Warren's oft-repeated aphorism is a worthy mantra for a local church; "a great commitment to the great commandment and the great commission will build a great church."[118]

Loving God and loving our neighbors involves reaching out in love, justice, and mercy to every accessible human being we may reach. It will be both local and global. Great churches wrestle with great issues. A renewed Methodism will be unafraid to confront issues of peace, economic injustice, racism, sexism, and the environment to mention but a few of the modern blights on human flourishing. Our understanding of Christian discipleship under the lordship (the sovereign rule) of Christ will be unflinchingly engaged in building a just society. It will do so in a manner and style not beholden to any political party or special interest group.

By way of example, during my (Bishop Lowry) service in the Central Texas Conference of the United Methodist Church we had a saying that stated: "If we are not actively addressing racism, we are not making disciples of Jesus Christ."[119] Going "back to the future," Methodist scholar Richard Heitzrater reminds us:

> "The Oxford Methodists in the early 1730s, nearly all university men, had spent a good deal of their time, money, and energy in a ministry of mercy to the poor – educating the children in the workhouses, taking food to the needy, providing wool and other materials from which people could make clothes and other durable goods to wear and sell. This particular emphasis on "love of neighbor" and following Christ's example ("who went about doing good," Acts 10:38). continued to characterize Methodism as it entered the revival."[120]

This great impetus for social justice has always been a hallmark of Methodism. For many clergies, the ministry is saturated by a justice and mercy impulse. This strong conviction to love God and love neighbor through ministries of love, justice and mercy is to be commended. This great gospel imperative will not be lost in a renewed Methodism. If a renewed Methodism is to be faithful to its Wesleyan mandate, it will insist on an understanding of sanctification that is both personal and corporate.[121] (It will also insist on an understanding of sin that is both individual and social.)

A reclaiming of the heart of the Christian faith will find a Global Methodist Church which will be insistent in fusing evangelism and missions of social justice under the Lordship Jesus Christ. The driver for social reform will not be a progressive indulgence of self-will and hedonism as a right but rather it will be driven by moral responsibility in faithfulness to God as Father, Son, and Holy Spirit.

By way of example, consider the dimensions of health care. While there may be a robust argument about how best to ensure proper health care for all, Christian faithfulness in a renewed Methodism will advocate healthcare for all as the responsibility of a just government. A renewed Methodism in the local church will reject concepts that reduce health care to the privilege of the financially well-off. Simultaneously, a renewed Methodism will move to join other Christians in rejecting abortion as a means of birth control. Passionately missional will move local churches beyond the static (and often morally obtuse) yoking of ethical issues with modern party politics.

These four pillars – 1) genuinely orthodox, 2) truly Wesleyan, 3) unapologetically evangelistic, and 4) passionately missional – of the local church in a renewed Methodism will be at the core recalling the heart of the Christian faith in the Global Methodist Church under the Lordship, the sovereign rule, of Jesus Christ. The renewed Methodism of the Global Methodist Church will not offer the two tablets from Mount Sinai to be taken with water. We will not proscribe a 12-step program to enforce on all congregations. Rather the Global Methodist Church will offer the core elements of a Wesleyan recovery for a way of faithfully being the church in the 21st century. "Going back to our Methodist future" will entail a long slow transition built on the four foundation pillars of local church integrity. Its bedrock will be built on Jesus Christ, fully human and fully divine. It will involve tough choices with steady wrestling over what it means to be in the world but not of it.

CHAPTER 7:
A RENEWED METHODISM IN THE LIFE OF THE LOCAL CHURCH

"For those who want to save their life will lose it, and those who lose their life for my sake, and for the sake of the gospel, will save it."
(Mark 8:35, NRSV)

We gathered on a Sunday in the late afternoon in September 2020. Despite the Texas heat, the setting was almost bucolic. We were spread out on a lake shoreline with a cooling copse of trees behind us. An anointed young couple, Jesus (pronounce Heyzus from the Spanish) and Lilly Molina had come from Venezuela with a calling to preach and teach in America. Since arriving in Texas, God had blessed them with the birth of their first child, a beautiful little girl named Paula who was now one year old.

On coming to America, they made their way first to Corsicana, Texas, where First United Methodist Church's custodian turned part-time local pastor discipled them into the Wesleyan way of being Christians. Moving to nearby Waxahachie, Texas, Jesus became the worship leader at First United Methodist Church's Spanish language service. The ministry continued to blossom. District Superintendent Rev. Leah Hidde-Gregory recruited them for a new faith community ministry as a part of a Covenant Parish of five churches reaching out to unreached people. The baptisms that night were the fruit of this new outreach ministry.

Today, this new faith community has expanded to a second site in Grapevine, Texas. Recently, in May 2022 (only a year and a half later) another baptism service was held in the lake. This time, 49 people, mostly adults, were baptized.

It is significant that the Covenant Parish (which is aided by First UMC Waxahachie) is made up primarily of Licensed Local Pastors who have a partial Course of Study School education. Only one of their leaders has a seminary education (a retired Elder who is more coordinator than boss). What they have instead is a sold-out commitment to Jesus Christ as Lord. The movement of the Holy Spirit transforming their lives is overwhelmingly present. Both individually and collectively they have known negative judgment and rejection. Together they intuitively experience Jesus liberating their lives. They speak easily, confidently, of the Holy Spirit moving in their lives.

As I waded into the water that Sunday evening in 2020 to share in the baptisms, five adults ranging in age from late teenagers to a person in their early 40s and one beautiful baby girl awaited us with excited expectation. With music, clapping, and cheers, the work of the Holy Spirit unfolded before us. This is a precursor, a hint of life in the local church in a renewed Methodism struggling to be born. It is deeply Holy Spirit lead, imbued with a transforming experience of Christ, and refreshingly reaching into new population groups. This scene would not be considered foreign or even unusual to early American Methodism. The Global Methodist Church is committed to a vision of life in renewed local congregations where such worship is common.

This ministry celebration is instructive of the future of a renewed Methodism in the local church which will be a Holy Spirit movement or stillborn. The lakeside setting reflects the nascent local church of a renewed Methodism in the Global Methodist Church reaching a combination of the middle class and working-class in its make-up. The UMC of today's United Methodism despite the best of intentions has taken on a college-educated, professional class culture and ethos. The future of Methodism does not stand for UMC = Upper Middle Class but without apology will embrace a working-class ethos and span multiple socio-economic & ethnic groups.

The building called "church" will not necessarily be the center of life in renewed Methodism nor will it even be the fixed locus of worship. Make no mistake, buildings are important and still needed but no longer will the primary focus revolve around maintaining a physical facility. Congregations that make the move from the UMC to the GMC with mistaken worship of their buildings will soon find themselves in a hospice situation. Building worship found in much of today's mainline Protestantism is not only idolatrous but a recipe for death.

The lakeside gathering reflects a church culture and ethos oriented around Jesus Christ and the Holy Spirit. At its best, the Global Methodist Church will be different from and ultimately reject a footprint defined either by culturally conservative republicanism or social justice democratic affiliation. This will not be easy. Under the Lordship of Jesus Christ guided by the inspiration of the Holy Spirit, our preferences and predilections will have to bow to His purposes. When we talk about Christ at the center, we really mean it!

It is the hope and prayer in the Global Methodist Church that life in the local church will reclaim an orthodox doctrine of the trinity moving away from a vague unitarian theological emphasis found in many of today's seminary-educated clergy. It will exhibit an openness to an expressive experience of the Holy Spirit (at times even Pentecostal in nature) which is foreign to a proper upper-middle-class church culture.

Key Elements of New Life in the Local Church

The elements of this lakeside gathering are almost reminiscent of John 21. They involve (at a minimum) seven elements that denote a marked change for the culturally mainline dying older version of Wesleyan witness:

1. Life transformation in, through, and under Jesus Christ (i.e. real conversion!),

2. a significantly new ethnic and cultural mix,

3. both a working class and a middle-class constituency,

4. a high Christology combined with a strong sense of biblical authority,

5. growing awareness of the power and the presence of the Holy Spirit,

6. indigenous leadership with spiritual and theological formation,

7. a firm commitment to historic Christian orthodoxy.

If the Covid-19 pandemic has taught us anything about life in the church today, it is taught us that our catechesis, that is our training in what it means to be Christian, is woefully inadequate. The Global Methodist Church will either return to the very heart of the Christian faith or it will be stillborn. Christian education and spiritual formation through the small group class structure will reclaim a central place in the life of spiritually healthy local churches. As we continue our slow transition into a post-Christian society, those who claim the name of Christ will repeatedly be challenged to gracefully yet firmly reject the dominant fads and fancies of contemporary culture regardless of whether they come from the left or right. (Dean Ing was right when he stated: "Whoever marries the spirit of this age will find himself a widower in the next."[122] Unfortunately, we have married the present age and it is past time for that to change.)

Faithful Practices

Built around the framework of the four pillars outlined in Chapter 6 (genuinely orthodox, truly Wesleyan, unashamedly evangelistic, and passionately missional), local churches of the Global Methodist Church will strive to exhibit a strong commitment to faithful practices yoked Wesleyan way of being Christian. Once again, they will earn the label of "methodical" (i.e., "Methodist") for faithfully being the local church.

First, the renewed Methodism in the local church will be far more **mission-driven**. Allegiance to Christ and advancing the

Kingdom of God will take precedent above personal preference or pleasure.[123] Apostolically the people and congregations of the dawn of a renewed Methodism are sent into the world by God for the sake of the world Christ came to save. In the local church, there will be a slow but steady recovery of a vibrant understanding of holiness of heart and life that is free from cultural correctness. Once again Methodism will be about reforming the nation, and in particular the church, while spreading scriptural holiness across the land.

Second, as already indicated, **discipled membership** will be limited to active practicing members of the community of faith. Congregations of the Global Methodist Church will be governed by committed disciples. The GMC will reject a "big tent" philosophy which is held captive by the lowest common denominator dictated by those who have joined for social appropriateness. Discipleship will be explicitly tied to discipline and biblical faithfulness. This will include an expectation for both faith sharing and hands-on ministry to the hurting, hungry, and homeless. While I (Bishop Lowry) was serving as Senior Pastor at University United Methodist Church in San Antonio, Texas, the Nominations and Leadership Committee instituted a policy of looking for some form of concrete evidence in the practice of prayers, presence, gifts, service, and witness in the life of those selected for leadership in the congregation. With a committee of 10 overlooking a membership of 5800+, we were still able to get a fairly accurate understanding of people's engagement in the basic practices of discipleship. Such a simple practice changed the dynamic of faithfulness in the governing Administrative Board.

Third, the practice of **small group discipleship** along the lines of the historic class and band meetings of Methodism will once again gain ascendancy in the life of the local church. Rod Dreher in *Live Not By Lies: A Manual For Christian Dissidents* repeatedly emphasizes the importance of small discipleship communities of faith. At one point he interviews Frantisek Miklosko, a sacrificial leader in the underground Slovak church during the time of communist persecution. Miklosko comments, "When I talk to young people today, … I tell them that what is crucial is to stay true to yourself, true to your conscience, and also to be in community with other like-minded people who share the faith. We were saved by small communities."[124] As America moves deeper into a post-Christian culture with battle lines between the so-called "woke" (what Dreher calls social justice cultists) and those enmeshed in alt-right preservation of white privilege and personal prosperity, it will be increasingly critical for those called Methodist Christians to share a gospel witness which offers a radically different witness of living in sacrificial Christ-like love for others. This can only happen with the re-emergence of some version of what were the original class meetings and small faith communities for formation, nurture, and spiritual refueling. It is well to be guided by Cyprian's (Bishop of Carthage in North Africa) remarks delivered to a struggling persecuted Christian community in 256 A.D. in a situation not that dis-similar to our own the early 21st Century America. "Beloved brethren," he wrote, "[we] are philosophers not in words but in deeds; we exhibit our wisdom not by our dress, but by truth; we know virtues by their practice rather than through boasting of them; we do not speak great things, but we live them."[125]

Fourth, **worship** will increasingly become a counter-cultural activity. The regular worship of God will once again become a defining characteristic of those who call themselves Christian. We can expect an increased emphasis on praise, historic affirmation including the use of the Creeds and regular communion, and an explicit sense of the Holy Spirit's presence.

The Dawn of New Life in the Local Church

Nowhere is there a clearer witness to the vision of the dawn of new life in the local church than that found in the life of William Wilberforce. While this Methodist layman is famously known for his lifelong battle to eradicate the slave trade in England, it is often forgotten that he was also engaged in several other moral justice issues confronting British society in the early days of Methodism. Under the more general rubric of "manners," Wilberforce worked for social reform on a wide variety of issues including advocacy for the rights of women. In words spoken as a eulogy, it was stated of him that

> "In an age and country fertile in great and good men,
> He was among the foremost of those who fixed the character of their times
> Because to high and various talents
> To warm benevolence, and to universal candour,
> He added the abiding eloquence of a Christian life."[126]

We invite the reader to consider prayerfully and carefully this last phrase, "the abiding eloquence of a Christian life." This is the audacious goal of the dawn of the Global Methodist Church both personally and collectively.

The church's transition to a renewed Methodism through the GMC will be rife with casualties and resplendent with fresh outbreaks of the Holy Spirit. When US Airways Flight 1549 began its emergency descent into the Hudson River after a bird strike, Captain Sully Sullenberger famously warned the passengers over the intercom "Brace for impact!" This warning begs to be shared as we transition to the GMC in the life of the local church. We have become too domesticated, too tempered in our reasoned response. It is time to remember again Hebrews 10:31. "It is a fearful thing to fall into the hands of the living God."[127]

Annie Dillard's pithy comment written decades ago still signals a demarcation line between a discipled community of faith and the pale imitation of the currently enculturated mainline imposter. "The churches are children [she wrote] playing on the floor with their chemistry sets, mixing up a batch of TNT to kill a Sunday morning. It is madness to wear ladies' straw hats and velvet hats to church; we should all be wearing crash helmets. Ushers should issue life preservers and signal flares; they should lash us to our pews. For the sleeping god may wake someday and take offense, or the waking god may draw us to where we can never return."[128] (O Lord, make it so!)

The dawning of a new age in Wesleyan movement of faith as represented by the Global Methodist Church will be both exciting and painful. It will not take place without genuine sacrifice. Institutionally, there will be dramatic changes. Local churches will initially get smaller (while some larger regional congregations will survive and thrive). The clergy culture of a guaranteed appointment is a "dead man walking." Whatever the final form of clergy placement, it will involve much greater involvement from the laity. Bishops will focus on their teaching ministry over and above managing the institution. Connectionalism for the local church will involve multiple-linked webs of missional relationships rather than a bureaucratic hierarchy. The institutional life of the Global Methodist Church will evolve with a dramatically smaller bureaucratic overhead. Counter-intuitively, there will be greater mission connection through local congregations voluntarily and often spontaneously joining together for disciple-making and mission outreach both locally and globally.

As a renewed Methodism struggles to be born in the Global Methodist Church, a part of the conflict will be a desire to nostalgically return to an earlier cultural ascendency (often heretically cloaked in the garb of conservative politics and distorted cultural wars). The shrill clamor of a politically perverted evangelicalism welded to a vituperative rearguard cultural war is a precursor to a religious train-wreck. As such, blind advocacy for conservative political values is a sinful millstone around the neck of an emerging post-Christendom Christian witness. At the same time, the emerging renewed Methodism will take on a different and altogether foreign hue from the progressive mainline UMC (United Methodist Church) with its obsessive commitment to liberal politics (especially on the part of the clergy union) and a culture of personal freedom welded to a distorted conception of inclusion divorced from a doctrine of personal holiness. The truth must be faced that the reward for cultural respectability of either the right or left has resulted in an emaciated church-man/woman-ship tragically lacking in allegiance to Christ and bereft of personal discipleship vigor.

Nominal Christianity will not survive in a post-Christendom climate, especially where the dominant cultural values of hedonistic materialism clash so egregiously with core Christian claims. Allegiance to Jesus Christ as both Lord and Savior must again be the heartbeat of living faith communities. The mission of making disciples of Jesus Christ[129] will/must gain greater clarity and specificity as disciple-making is strengthened.[130] The Global Methodist Church must be built, will be built, by congregations that consciously see themselves as mission posts of the advancing kingdom of God. They will move beyond the cultural minefield of a mainline Christianity consumed with issues of inclusion, multi-cultural egalitarianism, and economic socialism. They will reject the false piety of the heretical "prosperity gospel." They will eschew the clichéd therapeutic pampering of churches that honor the cross in principle yet pull back from the true meaning of sacrificial service and even suffering.

In her marvelous book *Teaching a Stone to Talk*, Annie Dillard recounts the story of the 1845 Sir John Franklin Expedition to find the northwest passage across the Arctic to the Pacific Ocean.[131] Peter Scazzero cogently summarizes the key background of this tragic expedition. The men of the Franklin Expedition "knew it would be a two-to-three-year journey, yet each sailing vessel carried only a twelve-day supply of coal. Instead of bringing more coal, each ship made room for a 1,200-volume library, a hand-organ playing fifty tunes, china place settings for officers and men, cut-glass wine goblets, and sterling silver flatware. They carried no special clothing for the Arctic except the uniforms of the Queen's Navy. When the Eskimos came across their frozen remains, the men were all dressed up, pulling a lifeboat full of sterling silver and chocolate."[132]

We as a people and a culture are like that. We are all dressed and frozen in place by the pursuit of lesser, petty gods. Our friends and neighbors, our nation and world, desperately need local churches of a renewed Methodism in the GMC sharing Christ to people frozen in place clutching at chocolate and silver. This is the task to which the Lord calls us.

Jesus said, "For those who want to save their life will lose it, and those who lose their life for my sake, and for the sake of the gospel, will save it."[133]

CHAPTER 8:
A VISION FOR THE GLOBAL METHODIST CHURCH—OR TEN REASONS WHY WE'RE EXCITED ABOUT AND WILL JOIN THE GLOBAL METHODIST CHURCH

*"Let anyone who has an ear listen to what
the Spirit is saying to the churches."
Revelation 3:22 (NRSV)*

As we write, we realize the journey into the Global Methodist Church is going to be easier for some than for others. What we had hoped could be a model for what it's like for Christians to disagree and go separate ways for the sake of the mission appears to have passed, and each annual conference of the United Methodist Church is setting its terms for congregations to withdraw or disaffiliate. Some are being gracious and have worked hard to live into the spirit of the proposed Protocol while others are being punitive and adding onerous criteria in an effort to hold congregations and clergy hostage to a church that doesn't want them any longer.

We realize congregations will be arriving at the Global Methodist Church in waves over the next few years and pray the General Conference of the United Methodist Church will find a way to be gracious in offering the terms for withdrawal or disaffiliation in the future. How we treat one another during these initial stages is vitally important. Some find themselves in a context where they need to get out while they can. Their context merits this action, and we yield to their understanding of their local situation. However, others are convinced the right move is to prepare for the next General Conference of the United Methodist Church and fight for something that reflects the spirit of the Protocol. Their context merits this decision, and we yield to their understanding of their local context.

This situation reminds me of an early meeting of the Wesleyan Covenant Association Global Council. In March of 2017, we had a fly-in meeting near the Hartsfield-Douglass International Airport in Atlanta. The agenda included meeting with several bishops, including some United Methodist bishops and some bishops from the Lutheran and Anglican Communions who were on the other side of their denominational conflicts. Another item on the agenda was that one of our council members had led his local church out of the United Methodist Church, and some members of the Council believed he needed to resign or be removed from the Council.

I (Jeff Greenway) remember the day well. The contrasts between the bishops could not have been more distinct. The United Methodist bishops looked the part. Dressed in suits with episcopal pins in clear view, they tried to appeal to the WCA Council that they knew the best way forward and that we should trust their guidance. The conversation was open and frank. I'm sure it did not go as they had planned.

The conversation with the Lutheran and Anglican bishops was entirely different. I walked away from the day with four clear impressions that shaped my leadership of the Council while I was the chair:

- They walked with a limp—meaning they had been through some extremely difficult, defining, and refining moments in their episcopal leadership that left them humble and approachable. They had paid a price for leading their respective organizations through schism and separation, and their humility was attractive and inspirational.

- They had reclaimed the teaching office of the episcopacy. They convinced us that doctrine matters, and the primary function of the episcopacy is to guard and defend the faith. Each of them was crystal clear about essentials and non-essentials when it came to the beliefs of their respective communions.

- They had reclaimed an evangelical urgency and church planting priority. They understood the new and exponential growth of new Jesus followers was not likely to happen through existing congregations—some of which smelled like the smoke of their denominational conflict and paid a heavy price for their freedom—but they convinced their new expressions to reclaim church planting as a priority.

- They reminded us that people would arrive at the future at different speeds and in different ways, but the way we treated them mattered. I believe it was an Anglican Bishop who said, "Be gracious with those who arrive early—and gentle with those who arrive late."

That last piece of advice was solid gold for the WCA Council. We didn't remove our brother who led his church out of the United Methodist Church early. We were gracious—then and now.

We believe that's still a good word for those who find themselves at different stages in the process of migrating from one denomination to another. Be gracious with those who arrive early and be gentle with those who arrive late. This will be our watchword and guide.

Every once in a while, and sometimes only once in a lifetime, we are given the opportunity to become involved in a life-changing, world-altering movement. Without resorting to hyperbole, we believe we are being given such an opportunity when joining the Global Methodist Church. This is an incredible moment in history, and we believe God has given us the opportunity to partner with Him and other like-minded, warm-hearted, Jesus-loving, Spirit-filled, Wesleyan, orthodox Christians to a new part of a New Methodism for the 21st Century which is deeply rooted on global

Christianity while leaning forward to share the Gospel with people in desperate need of its saving and sanctifying grace.

Let us be clear, the Global Methodist Church will not be United Methodism 2.0. If you think this is just about changing the name on the front of your church building without being intentional about embedding distinctively Wesleyan DNA in your congregation—don't come. While we shared an initial disappointment that the Judicial Council of the UMC ruled Annual Conferences cannot vote to leave on their own, we have come to believe that the Global Methodist Church will be stronger and more vibrant if we're made up of congregations and pastors who have counted the cost of joining this movement.

Friends, the time has come for us to reclaim our theological roots, rediscover the practices that fueled the Methodist revival, and stop fighting so we can beat our swords into plowshares and start planting the seeds for a new expression of Methodism. We can live into a new and renewed future—to reclaim and live out the powerful DNA that propelled John Wesley and the first Methodists to take the Gospel to the world and spread Scriptural holiness across the land. We know that no great movement of God has come without great sacrifice, determination, and faith from God's people—and that will likely be the case for us. Salvation is free—but discipleship is costly.

We write this knowing not everyone reading this or the congregations they represent will be able or choose to withdraw or disaffiliate from the United Methodist Church. We get it. For some, it will be a bridge too far or a price too high.

In Matthew's Gospel, Jesus said, "If anyone would come after me—he must deny himself—take up his cross and follow me. For whoever would save his life will lose it—and whoever loses his life for my sake and the Gospel's—will find it."[134] We believe we're at a cross-carrying/life-losing crossroads.

Perhaps what God is asking us to do is to deny ourselves, our plans, our terms, our buildings, and the security and cover the Protocol afforded—and take up our cross, step forward in faith, and follow Him. We believe it is so and invite the reader to engage in deep prayerful discernment. Who's with us?

Here are our top ten reasons we recommend you consider joining the Global Methodist Church.

1. Consistent Faithfulness in Doctrine

What we believe matters. It was with great intention we named our new book of order The Doctrines and Discipline. We wanted to move our basic beliefs from being merely historic and suggestive documents—to authoritative standards that are a source of doctrinal authority and spiritual integrity. Our doctrinal beliefs and practice are rooted in historic Christianity and will keep us connected and in step with the global big "C" Church of Jesus Christ. Rather than continuing to approach scripture, doctrine, and practice from a place of skepticism and syncretism, we look forward to working with people who hold the same view of scripture, doctrine, and practice.

At a recent WCA Global Gathering (we are indebted to the work the Wesleyan Covenant Association has done behind the scenes preparing for the birth of the Global Methodist Church!), a younger pastor told me (Jeff Greenway) how refreshing it was for him to be in a room of Methodist where he didn't need to wonder what the words meant when they were being used. He remarked that the resurrection was accepted and declared as a historic reality rather than as a metaphor or allegory. He also observed how quickly the body elected a new class of WCA to the WCA Global Council that was balanced and representative in gender, race, nationalities, and age. We look forward to the day when doctrinal unity and orthodox conviction strip away many of the differences that have divided us in the past.

2. Reclaim Accountable Discipleship

When Methodism has and currently is taking the world by storm, accountable discipleship was its basic unit. The class and band meetings of Methodism were the places where lives were transformed through accountable discipleship. The church I (Jeff Greenway) serve in Reynoldsburg, Ohio was formed 190 years ago. It began as a Methodist class meeting in a local blacksmith shop along the creek that runs through our community.

When Methodism was sweeping across the United States, and where it is sweeping across countries and regions today, it's often rooted in small groups exercising accountable discipleship. Many of the United Methodist Churches located across the United States today were class meetings formed when the Methodists were adding "a church a day" in the 1840s. One of the things that slowed our prior growth was the establishment of the Sunday School—a more informational model of discipleship—instead of the class meeting—which was a more transformational model.

The convening conference of the Global Methodist Church will be considering participation in an accountable discipleship group as a requirement for church membership. We believe a reclamation of this important, historical part of our DNA will be one of the keys to moving us forward.

3. Church Planting

The Transitional Leadership Council of the Global Methodist Church has embraced the goal of launching 3,500 new communities of faith in the next seven years. This will not be generated out of District or Conference offices, but rather out of local churches. This is already taking place in parts of the Methodist movement which are going on outside North America. In the United States, new church starts will learn from places like the Philippines and Africa. These new communities of faith will not likely be parachute drops or start with a large investment of resources, but rather, using early Methodist DNA and some of the house church and micro-church models developed by organizations like Exponential and Fresh Expressions, we will be launching churches that look more like class meetings than brick and mortar edifices reflecting the past. We believe this will be an important aspect of reclaiming our disciple-making DNA from our past which will launch us into our future.

4. Mission Driven Rather than Structurally Bound

Purposeful systems and structures are important ways we move forward, but the United Methodist Church presently has 13 General Boards and Agencies that are drowning in their bureaucracy.

In contrast, during the last five years, over 1,000 volunteers have worked to put together recommendations on mission partnerships, accountable discipleship, church multiplication, ministry in the margins, and a host of other initiatives—without the encumberment of a bloated structure. It's amazing what the Spirit can do if we get out of the way.

We believe the Global Methodist Church will resist bureaucracy and organize itself in flexible, fluid commissions that will do most of their work virtually using the technologies we all learned to use through the recent pandemic—which will enable much more diverse, creative, and economically viable participation in the denomination's system while keeping it lean and nimble.

5. Term-Limited Episcopacy

Historically, Methodist bishops were never intended to be a class of "super-elders," but the reality is the Council of Bishops of the United Methodist Church has acted as such. We (Bishop Mike Lowry and Jeff Greenway) have different views of what the episcopacy should look like, a view anchored in the biblical and early Christian model of the episcopacy.

I (Jeff Greenway) chaired the initial task team that developed the first draft of the Doctrine and Discipline, and one of the early conversations we had was whether to eliminate the episcopacy. We decided we believe having bishops is historically important but have made some recommended changes that will need to be affirmed by the convening Conference of the Global Methodist Church. We recommend the elimination of jurisdictional conferences (which are the residue of institutional racism and the source of the move to regionalized expressions of faith in the United Methodist Church), and that bishops be elected at the General Conference. We recommended bishops be elected for a maximum 12-year term, and if the bishop is not of retirement age, their title is "Bishop Emeritus" when their term ends, and they return to serve a local church. We strongly recommend a redefinition of the episcopacy from that of institutional maintenance and leadership—to reclaiming the teaching office of the church.

We've also separated the spiritual and temporal responsibilities of United Methodist Bishops. The role the of Bishop in the

Global Methodist Church will be primarily spiritual —teaching the faith, ordaining clergy, and fixing appointments—but the operational leadership of the more temporal affairs will be delegated to a Connectional Operating Officer. The Connectional Operating Officer will be hired by and accountable to the bishops but will provide day-to-day leadership to the temporal operations of the denomination. This will free the bishops for intentional and robust spiritual leadership (a leadership which we believe the church desperately needs!).

I (Jeff Greenway) use a model like this in the local church I serve. As Lead Pastor, I'm the primary spiritual leader of our congregation and am charged with teaching the faith, administering the sacraments, and ordering the life of the church—but the details of operational leadership are handled primarily by an Executive Director (finance and property) and Executive Pastor (ministry staff and missional ministries). While I set the direction of the overall mission and ministry of our congregation, I rarely get involved in day-to-day operations.

I (Bishop Lowry) believe it is time to lay aside the Judicial Council structure and ask bishops to once again lead the church and not simply manage (and protect) the institution. Bishops are to be "overseers."[135] Bishops would have the responsibility to rule on church discipline. A simple review could be instituted to check any attempt at abuses of power.

As you can see, while a few of the details are still to be decided by the convening conference of the Global Methodist Church, the proposals being placed before it calls for a redefined episcopacy. We (Dr. Jeff Greenway and Bishop Emeritus Mike Lowry) have own differences about the future shape of the episcopacy. This will be a time of discernment and learning for all as we seek the will and guidance of the Holy Spirit. What we are firmly united in is a yearning for the day when our bishops are servants committed to guarding and defending the faith rather than institutional bureaucrats leading us away from it.

6. Systemic Accountability

The Global Methodist Church is committed to systemic accountability. When I (Jeff Greenway) was leading the team that drafted the first proposal for the Doctrines and Discipline, there was a short time when we were attempting to write a polity that was reacting to everything we were experiencing in the United Methodist Church. We quickly got bogged down and could have easily spent so much time articulating what we're against or moving from—that we would lose sight of what we're being called to. We finally decided we can't build a system that prevents bad actors or ineffectiveness, but we could build one that makes it easy to remove them.

We believe one of the reasons the United Methodist Church is in a constitutional crisis is because those who were charged with guarding and defending the faith and holding us accountable to our common covenant, are not accountable themselves. The Global Methodist Church will exhibit covenantal accountability at every level—including an accountability system for bishops that is not controlled by bishops.

7. Lean Bureaucracy—Lower Costs—No Trust Clause

While there needs to be some systemic structure to the new denomination, those planning for the launch of the Global Methodist Church have been intentional in planning for a lean bureaucracy. We don't envision a top-heavy, centrally controlled denominational system that gets hung up in in survival. We dream of a church that is a movement and gives permission for multiple structures, systems, and mission partners.

We will have a convening conference in the near future which will likely be followed by another General Conference in short order, but the goal is to hold a General Conference every six years. We don't envision General Boards and Agencies populated and controlled by ministry insiders, but rather Commissions served primarily by volunteers who use the technology we've discovered during the pandemic to provide policy leadership to the initiatives of the church.

One result of this leaner structure will be lower denominational costs. While most United Methodist congregations currently contribute up to 15% of their income (minus mortgage and mission-related funds) for apportionments, the Global Methodist Church will begin with a shared ministry of 2% of their income (minus mortgage and mission-related expenses) with a maximum of 6.5%[136]—which can only be changed by a super-majority of the General Conference. The goal is to keep more resources in the local church for mission and ministry. At the time of this writing, the Transitional Leadership Council has signaled an initial period with minimal shared ministry funding to allow local churches the opportunity to restore some of the resources lost by having to fulfill the costs for disaffiliation in each annual conference.

The Global Methodist Church will not have a trust clause. While the history of the trust clause was to maintain sound doctrine, our recent history in the United Methodist Church is the trust clause was used to keep a dysfunctional church together. The Global Methodist Church intends to be a movement of the compelled rather than a prison for the constrained.

8. More Congregational Input on Clergy Selection

Gone will be the days when churches and pastors are not consulted and engaged in the clergy selection and assignment process. A major step in developing a system of clergy deployment that has significant input from the laity in churches receiving a pastor and clergy accepting a new assignment will be the abolition of the "guaranteed appointment." In truth, the guaranteed appointment is, in Bishop Lowry's terms, a "dead-man walking," in both the United Methodist Church and the Global Methodist Church. It is simply no longer financially sustainable. Furthermore, the abolition of the guaranteed appointment will, we believe, be a significant move in the direction of developing effective clergy. One of the most distasteful aspects of my (Bishop Lowry) work as a UMC Bishop was the need to appoint people to local churches who were not effective or competent. It is time for the clergy union as a protective association to end. Simultaneously, the GMC must and will be dedicated to putting in place systems that protect and enhance appointment making across gender and ethnic lines.

The convening conference of the GMC will be considering a modified call system for clergy deployment. While neither of us knows the final shape that modified call system will take, we can imagine a system where Presiding Elders will work with the lay leadership of a church to put together a short list of recommended possibilities (perhaps 5). The laity will have the ability to add to that list if desired. The final appointment placement will evolve by common agreement between the Supervising Elder, pastor, and congregation with the bishop retaining a veto in unusual situations.

9. Easier Path to Ordination

The present path to ordination in the UMC is a long one. It is often not attained until long after a person has invested up to ten years and thousands of dollars in educational training. To that end, we envision a much more careful system of local church examination and endorsement of someone as a candidate for ordained ministry. Yoked with the abolition of the "guaranteed appointment," we seek close cooperation between conferences and seminaries. With strong local church endorsement of candidates for ordination, it is possible to move towards a system of clergy training and development which simultaneously does not leave seminary graduates with excessive debt and renders a much higher ability and spiritual development for new clergy seeking pastoral assignments.

The proposed path to ordination in the GMC reclaims the historic nesting of ministry with the ordering of licensed and ordained ministry flowing out of the ministry of the Baptized, exemplified and set apart in the ministry of word and service as a Deacon, and refined and set a part of the ministry of word, sacrament, and order as an Elder. The paths of ordination through seminary or the course of study will result in full clergy membership for persons serving the Global Methodist Church. Our goal is to rid ourselves of the unhealthy clergy caste system of the past and fully celebrate the ministry of the baptized and the called.

10. Global from Day One

The next few years will see the churches and pastors migrate from the UMC to the GMC in waves. The first wave of existing and new churches has come during this last Annual Conference season, and we believe waves will come in December of 2022, the summer of 2023, December of 2023, and if/when the UM General Conference makes a pathway to amicable separation possible when the proposed General Conference meets in April of 2024.

That said, the initial wave of churches and clergy joining the GMC are coming from around the world—the Bulgaria Annual Conference, groups of newly forming churches from regions in Africa, existing congregations in the Philippines, existing congregations from various conferences in the US, new church starts, and networks of house churches in regions of the US.

We've also been in regular communication with existing Wesleyan denominations from around the world who are interested in exploring ways we may be able to partner in mutually beneficial ways.

As we work together with the Transitional Leadership Council, we are impressed with the strength and contributions of our global partners in vision-casting and decision-making. As the General Commissions (populated by volunteer servants) are being connected technologically to begin to operationalize the lean and nimble denominational structure, great care is being given to giving equal voice and autonomy to all regions of the GMC. We do not want to repeat some of the paternalistic patterns of the past, and are working hard to give each regional expression of our movement the creative autonomy to organize and flourish while maintaining the theological and covenantal core that is essential for our movement,

We wish to strongly reiterate; the Global Methodist Church will not be United Methodism 2.0. We write to invite you to prayerfully consider joining a dynamic movement of like-minded, warm-hearted, Jesus-loving, Wesleyan, evangelical, orthodox, and covenant-keeping Christians who are connected in mission. United in Christ, we are committed to sharing the gospel in both word and deed for the sake of the bruised and battered world our Lord came to save.

We ask that people don't just come to the GMC because they're looking for something new or hoping to save money on apportionments or any other base motive. We do not offer a utopian version of the Kingdom come to earth. We often tell people looking for the perfect church not to join one when they find it—because it won't be perfect anymore! Together we offer Christ and Him crucified![137] We remind all: "The message of the cross is foolishness to those who are being destroyed. But it is the power of God for those of us who are being saved."[138]

CHAPTER 9:
PIONEERS OF A NEW CHURCH

"Therefore, since it is by God's mercy that we are engaged
in this ministry, we do not lose heart."
2 Corinthians 4:1 (NRSVUE)

Lately, we've been reflecting on what it means to be a pioneer in a movement like the Global Methodist Church. As we've done so, we've drawn strength, encouragement, and insight from the New Testament and Church history.

John chapter 16, records portions of Jesus' conversations with his followers on the last night of his life. Jesus knew he was about to walk the way to the cross—leaving his disciples when he said: "It is better for you that I go away because if I don't, the advocate (paraclete) won't come."[139] The Greek word *"paraclete"* means "called to one's side to encourage, uphold, assist, and HELP." The Holy Spirit is a helper sent to encourage, uphold and assist the Church, and help us lift the cause of the Kingdom of God.

Later that night, Jesus was arrested—beaten—and condemned. Jesus was crucified, dead, and buried—and on the third day, Jesus rose from the dead. The Gospel of John ends with the risen and living Jesus appearing to his disciples.

On the next page, in Acts chapter 1, Jesus said, "Do not leave Jerusalem until the Father sends you what he promised. Remember I have told you about this before. John baptized with water, but in just a few days I will baptize with the Holy Spirit." Jesus was leaving the earth so the Holy Spirit would come.

The disciples stayed in Jerusalem—they waited and prayed. Ten days later, they were having a prayer service, and it was interrupted by the "sound of a rushing wind" and the Holy Spirit arrived in the form of tongues of fire—settling upon the people in the room. At that moment, the big "C" Church was born.

As we read the Acts of the Apostles, it becomes clear that the person of Jesus who was limited by his physical body is now gone, but in his place is the unlimited and pulsating Holy Spirit. The Holy Spirit was everywhere at once—and the era of the Spirit-filled Church began.

Acts chapter 4 gives us a glimpse of what it was like: "All the believers were united in heart and mind. And they felt that what they owned was not their own, so they shared everything they had. The apostles testified powerfully to the resurrection of the Lord Jesus, and God's great blessing was upon them all."[140] And they all lived happily ever after, right? Wrong! Acts chapter 5 opens with the story of Ananias and Sapphira who were struck dead because they lied to the Holy Spirit. Acts chapter 6 shows factions of the Church fighting over the fair distribution of food to their widows. Isn't it fascinating that the first two problems to hit the fledgling church were hypocrisy and injustice? Don't we all long to leave those sins behind!

The rest of the New Testament tells the dynamic story of the Church which most historians believe grew from 120 at Pentecost to hundreds of thousands in fifty years. Yet, despite great success in spreading the Gospel, an unsettling undercurrent runs throughout the whole of the New Testament: There are problems in the church. Some come from the outside—that's to be expected. But the most serious are those that come from within. That's troubling, but it still happens today, which raises the question: If the Church is God's plan to carry out the ministry of Jesus, why is it so messed up? The short answer is because it's filled with people—like you and me!

The Second Letter to the Corinthians was written by Paul to one of the most dysfunctional churches in the New Testament.

But in the first nine verses of the chapter, we find six solid pieces of advice for those who want to live into the fullness of being a part of the big "C" Church while living in the small "c" church.

1. Don't Lose Heart

"Therefore, since through God's mercy we have this ministry, we DO NOT LOSE HEART."[141]

Never give up the ministry God has given us. The ministry God has given the big "C" Church is to carry on the ministry of Jesus Christ: to turn non-believers into believers, to turn believers into the disciples, and to turn disciples into leaders. At the church I (Jeff Greenway) serve, we call this spiritual development. We have plans and intentionality in helping people cross the line of faith to become spiritual infants, grow to become spiritual adolescents, and mature to become spiritual parents. If this was easy, everyone would be doing it. It's not. It's hard work, but it's what we do. And although the work is often difficult, we must not grow discouraged or weary in the work.

2. Tell the Truth

"Rather, we have renounced secret and shameful ways; we do not use deception, nor do we distort the Word of God. On the contrary, by setting forth the truth plainly we commend ourselves to everyone's conscience in the sight of God."[142]

We must be above reproach in every way if we are to reflect God's glory to the world. Think of the church as a mirror that reflects the radiance of God. There is nothing we can add to the radiance of God—we just have to keep the mirror clean. Unethical churches and pastors throw mud on the mirror and mud can't reflect anything. Let's be careful to keep the mirror of our lives clean so that we can reflect God's glory to the world. This is the work of sanctifying grace which is the crown of our Wesleyan tradition.

It will take discipline and intentionality to reintroduce a Wesleyan understanding of being made perfect in love (sanctification) into our DNA. We're coming from a place where sin has infiltrated the system to the point it is often not recognized any longer as it demands to be accepted. As a result, the reflection of the "church" the world often sees looks more like the world than a redeemed, forgiven, holy and loving church. We need to reclaim the ability to name sin while announcing grace and calling each other to robust and attractive holiness. This is not holiness that centers on what we're against, but rather one that reflects what we're for as we're saved to the uttermost.

3. Love the Lost

"And even if our gospel is veiled, it is veiled to those who are perishing. The god of this age has blinded the minds of unbelievers so that they cannot see the light of the gospel that displays the glory of Christ, who is the image of God."[143]

Satan has blinded the minds of many in our world and sometimes in the church, and they are unable to see God's light. They have not been awakened. They don't understand the message we preach. Paul does not let the Corinthian church vilify those who are not ready to accept the Gospel because he knows the church won't reach people we do not love. Evil invites judgment, but blindness invites compassion.

I (Jeff Greenway) recently had a conversation with an experienced teacher who gave me a dose of reality when it comes to transformational learning. She told me some students catch on to learning right away. Other students come along and begin learning after a while. And still, others never get it. For the last group, there was only one thing a teacher can do—keep teaching to the best of their ability. Paul kept on preaching because he loved the lost—so should we!

4. Preach Jesus by Serving

"For what we preach is not ourselves, but Jesus Christ as Lord, and ourselves as your servants for Jesus' sake."[144]

For Paul, Christian leadership was always about service. He shook off rejection, rejected entitlement, endured ridicule, preached Jesus with courage, and survived beatings in service to Jesus and His church. Jesus taught that we become rich by giving, live by dying, and the greatest are the servants of all. When Jesus demonstrated greatness, he washed his disciple's feet. The church is here to serve, not to be served.

When I (Jeff Greenway) was a college student, I worked on a large regional evergreen farm. During those years, I learned the difference between positional and ascribed authority. The owner's son was the "boss" of our work crew. He showed up every morning in his shiny red pick-up truck with the company insignia painted on the doors, would meet us in the loading dock, and give us our orders for the day. Warm and hot days were spent planting, digging, or hoeing mile-long rows of evergreens or getting the bailed hay from the fields into the several barns the company owned. Hot and rainy days were spent cleaning horse stalls and cow pens. It was noble, back-straining work that served as a reminder of why I wanted to get my education.

Our "boss" would give us the orders, get in his truck, and we never saw him again. It had been years since he handled a hoe or threw a bale of hay. He had all the positional authority in the world, but he wasn't the leader. The leader—the one who earned our loyalty and trust—was an older man named Eddie. He had worked at this job for 30 years. His back was bent. His hands were calloused. No one moved until Eddie picked up his hoe, and said, "Come on boys!" He worked with us. He made sure we had water. He taught us how to pace ourselves in the heat. He was—there! In a real way, he was the first to show me what servant leadership looks like. It's a leadership that models as it serves—not one that pontificates from a distance.

The leadership that will bring the GMC into the future with a sense of hope and purpose will not rely upon positional authority but will gladly take a towel and basin while modeling approachable servanthood.

5. Remember what the Treasure is

"For God, who said, 'Let light shine out of darkness,' made his light shine in our hearts to give us the light of the knowledge of God's glory displayed in the face of Christ. But we have this treasure in jars of clay to show that this all-surpassing power is from God and not from us."[145]

Paul reminds us that we have been given a treasure, but this precious treasure. this light and power that shine within us, is held in the clay pots of our imperfect lives.

121

I (Jeff Greenway) have a friend who collects old baseball cards. His favorite is a 1933 Goudey card of St. Louis Cardinal great Dizzy Dean. He keeps his card encased in a thick screw-down plastic case, but it is not the case that determines the value of the card. If the case got beat up, dinged, cracked, vandalized, and scarred, it would not detract from the value of the card one cent. The case isn't important—the card is. This is what Paul declares and we affirm: "But we have this treasure in jars of clay to show that this all-surpassing power is from God and not from us."[146] The Gospel of Jesus Christ is the card and local churches are the cases. We are the clay pot that contains priceless treasure! This way people can see that anything good we do comes from God. When we remember that is not about us—reflect the light of God to the world, and effectively carry the treasure of the Gospel, the world will know that what we do comes from God.

6. Never Give Up

"We are hard pressed on every side, but not crushed; perplexed, but not in despair; persecuted, but not abandoned; struck down, but not destroyed."[147]

We are pressed, but not crushed. We are discouraged, but we do not quit. We get knocked down, but we get back up and keep on pressing forward.

When I (Jeff Greenway) was a District Superintendent, I received word that the pastor in one of the churches I was responsible for had an inappropriate relationship with a woman in his congregation. As the news poured in, it went from bad to worse to worse than that. He was removed due to moral and ethical failings. It broke my heart and the hearts of the people who trusted and believed in him.

Did this reveal something about the character of that pastor? Absolutely! Did this testify to a fallen world? Absolutely! Did this destroy my belief in the Church of Jesus Christ? Absolutely not! We worked with the leadership of that congregation and found another pastor who would come, bring healing and provide solid leadership. Were we pressed? Yes, but we were not crushed. Were we discouraged? Yes, but we did not quit. Were we knocked down? Yes, but we got back up! Serving God in a fallen world is not for the faint of heart, but we are not the faint of heart. We are the Church of Jesus Christ. We believe God is good. We understand bad things happen, but we will do everything we can to press on.

This is hard to grasp, but how we react to situations like this is determined by the maturity of commitment to the relationship and the stability of our covenant. As local church pastors, we are committed to helping couples keep their commitments when it comes to the covenant of marriage. In a world where marriages are often treated as contracts made to be broken, we have worked hard to help each couple we've married to keep their covenant commitment to each other and the Lord. We've sat with couples in the darkest of times, but when they're committed to their relationship and want to work to keep or mend their covenant, it's an amazing thing to watch!

However, we've also seen occasions when the covenant of trust has been broken so severely that the only salvageable parts of the relationship are the individual parts. It's almost like both parties are careening out of control in a slow-motion accident while inflicting untold harm on each other. We take no joy in situations like this, but when the covenant is broken, it's impossible to repair without work and commitment from both parties. Divorce becomes inevitable because trust cannot be restored.

One other truth we've learned is that distrust from broken marriage covenants has the potential to impact future marriage relationships. Second marriages often come apart because the people who enter them haven't done the heart work to recognize that the "intense fellowship" in their new marriage is not the same as what led to the end of their last marriage, and often, in self-preservation, they leave the relationship to guard their hearts and even souls from further pain.

A relationship with a church is no different than a relationship with a person. Sadly, we find ourselves walking out of a denomination where covenant and trust have been broken. As we've previously stated, the UMC has become ungovernable, and we barely recognize the people we used to share covenant with. For us, it feels like an ecclesiastical divorce, and the irreconcilable differences among us have resulted in our need to be in separate churches—but in the process, we have some heart work to do. As we press on, we will need to commit ourselves to work on our new covenant relationships while not continually having flashbacks to the old because some people cycle through after church the same way people cycle through relationship after relationship.

There are five Stages of Church Commitment—that apply to local congregations and denominations:

1. NEW—"This is the perfect church."

When we are new to a church, we think: "This is the perfect church! I am going to give it my all!" You and I know this is not realistic. There are no perfect churches and if you ever find one, you will ruin the whole thing the moment you show up. This sense of newness is temporary because it is essentially based upon an illusion. The perfect church does not exist.

2. CONFUSION—"This church isn't perfect."

Before long, we get confused about a church and think: "What, this church isn't perfect!?" When the balloon of our honeymoon at a church is popped by reality, we're temporarily disoriented and stunned. The fact that this happens is stunning in itself but it happens—and happens—and happens.

3. DISENCHANTMENT—"I thought this was a perfect church..."

This is the point at which people say, "I have been hurt by the church." The church isn't whatever that person thought it would be or should be and they are brought to a crisis point.

4. DECISION—"I am going to quit this church and look for a perfect church" or "I am going to realize that no church is perfect and serve God anyway."

We want to be very clear: some churches are toxic and getting out is the right move. We believe this is exactly where we are with the dysfunction of the United Methodist Church. If you want to be healthy and functional, don't stay within a dysfunctional church. But let me give a word of caution: if we are too quick to hit the eject button every time the plane ride gets bumpy, we are sure going to crash a lot of planes on one hand and never learn to pilot in bad weather on the other.

Here is the deal: even highly effective churches consist of flawed people, flawed systems, and flawed leaders because we live in a flawed and fallen world. Sometimes leaving is the right answer, but much more often the right play is to stay and be a part of making something better.

The final stage is:

5. MATURITY—"This is an imperfect church!! But it is MY church, and I will give it my all!"

Those who grow to this point get ALL the benefits of loving their church, but they are now in a sustainable position to serve effectively for the long haul. They don't expect that things will be easy, systems will be flawless, and people will never make mistakes. It was with people like this that Jesus Christ built his big "C" Church and for folks like this the Holy Spirit came at Pentecost!

There have been many times we've wondered if the priceless treasure was in there at all, or if it was just a clay pot. We've had dry seasons of discouragement, disappointment, and heartache, but to miss the priceless treasure because we are discouraged by the clay pot would be like throwing away a Dizzy Dean card because the plastic case is scratched. What keeps mature people of faith going is a sharp focus on the treasure and not the container.

You may be thinking, "I've been hurt by the church." Me, too! You might say, "The church is full of hypocrites!" No doubt about it! You might cry, "Christians have let me down!" I get that! You might conclude," "I don't believe in organized religion." Me neither. The big "C" Church of Jesus Christ doesn't exist for the organization of religion—it exists to help people connect with Jesus. Period.

Christianity is a relationship, not a religion. The little "c" church is an imperfect institution run by imperfect people who are endeavoring to carry on the ministry of a perfect Savior. We're going to fall short from time to time and even have stuff blow up—it goes without saying. But the big "C" Church is God's strategy for bringing the Good News of Jesus to the world, and God is going to work through the Church of Jesus Christ with or without organized religion, United Methodism, your local church, you or me.

Why? Because the Church is of God and will be preserved to the end of time—for the conduct of worship, the due administration of His word and sacrament, the maintenance of Christian fellowship and discipline, the edification of believers, and the conversion of the world.

If the invitation is on the table for us to be a part of what God is doing on planet Earth through the big "C" church, we're in--clay pot and all. What about you? You see we've read the back of the book. When the smoke clears, when the dust settles, when darkness is vanquished by light, the Kingdom comes with the sounds of trumpets, the Church of Jesus Christ will reign victorious forever and ever and ever and ever. And on that day, the priceless will be bound by the earthen vessel no more and we can live into the Kingdom of God! Until then—we have the Church.

AN INVITATION

"Yet whatever gains I had, these I have come to regard as loss because of Christ. More than that, I regard everything as loss because of the surpassing value of knowing Christ Jesus my Lord. For his sake I have suffered the loss of all things, and I regard them as rubbish, in order that I may gain Christ and be found in him, not having a righteousness of my own that comes from the law but one that comes through faith in Christ, the righteousness from God based on faith. I want to know Christ and the power of his resurrection and the sharing of his sufferings by becoming like him in his death, if somehow I may attain the resurrection from the dead. Not that I have already obtained this or have already reached the goal, but I press on to lay hold of that for which Christ has laid hold of me. Brothers and sisters, I do not consider that I have laid hold of it, but one thing I have laid hold of: forgetting what lies behind and straining forward to what lies ahead, I press on toward the goal, toward the prize of the heavenly call of God in Christ Jesus.
(Philippians 3:7-14, NSRV)

There is a vividly gripping scene recounted by Stephen Ambrose in *Undaunted Courage*. The crew of the Corps of Discovery had left St. Louis. They had wintered in Fort Mandan on the Missouri River in present-day North Dakota. Come spring, they continued up the Missouri River crossing into Montana and arriving at Lemhi Pass. The conventional wisdom of their day held that as they crossed the pass, they would find themselves on a gradually descending downward slope to the Pacific Ocean. Climbing the pass, they thought their journey was near an end. Instead, they discovered the Bitterroot Mountain Range which lay ahead and a dangerous trek over the Lolo Trail beyond. The temptation to turn back must have been overwhelming.

They did not turn back. They did not give up. They pressed on eventually stumbling into a tribe of friendly Nez Perce Indians in present-day Idaho. History records that the Nez Perce took care of them and nursed them back to health. They lost only one life, and that happened earlier on the trip and was because of a medical issue. The great voyage of discovery reached the Pacific Ocean.

Something like this may serve as an analogy for what we face in the dawning of a new Wesleyan /witness of faith. Leaving the United Methodist Church means leaving the protection of a comfortable risk-averse institution. Moving to a new denomination involves courageously blazing a trail to a new future of faithfulness in building the Kingdom of God. For those of you considering such a step, we offer seminal advice.

As we peer into an uncertain future, it is important to remind ourselves that we have been here before. Periodically throughout the long history of the church and the larger Christian movement, those who follow Christ have faced difficult decisions. We can gain wisdom and guidance by looking at what has gone before. We know the old phrase "the main thing is to keep the main thing the main thing."

The church does not belong to us. It is Christ's church. Biblically speaking, the church is the body of Christ.[148] Our ultimate allegiance does not lead us to institutional safety nor does it lead us to unity at all costs. Our ultimate security lies in following Christ. We are a pilgrim people.

The Apostle Paul's word to the infant church at Philippi applies to us today. "Yet whatever gains I had, these I have come to regard as loss because of Christ. More than that, I regard everything as loss because of the surpassing value of knowing Christ Jesus my Lord."[149] The Global Methodist Church will live out of a deep commitment to Jesus Christ as Lord. Paul's phrase, "I press on toward the goal, toward the prize of the heavenly call of God in Christ Jesus."[150] serves as an altar call for a move to a new Wesleyan movement of faith represented by the Global Methodist Church.

I (Bishop Lowry) have a phrase I shared over and over again in the Central Texas Conference as we went through the deep struggles leading to separation. "Breathe deep, Jesus is still Lord!" The heart of faithfulness lies in this cardinal affirmation. A friend of mine reports riding with another pastor to a meeting one day. The pastor drove so fast and so recklessly that my friend exclaimed, "Bishop, I discovered new dimensions of prayer and rededicated my life to Jesus four times on the drive." Behind the humor lies a truth that we wish to impress upon the reader. This time, this decision, and this move, calls for deep prayer, patient spiritual discernment, ardent listening to the Holy Spirit, and most of all rededicated allegiance to Jesus as Lord. Truly, "they who wait upon the Lord shall renew their strength!"[151]

If you find yourself yearning for the kind of expression of the church we've been describing in the pages of this book, we invite you to join us as we make our way into the Global Methodist Church. We have no illusion it will be easy, but following Jesus rarely is. While we have clear pilings in the ground upon which to build and support this movement, we need the experience, spiritual energy, and faithfulness of people like you to help us live into the promise this movement holds. We invite you to join us and other like-minded, warm-hearted, Jesus- loving, Wesleyan, evangelical, orthodox, and covenant-keeping Christians who are connected in mission.

We have the opportunity to live into a new and renewed future—to reclaim and live out the powerful DNA that propelled John Wesley and the first Methodists to take the Gospel to the world and spread Scriptural holiness across the land—and we invite you to join us!

As we seek the leading of the Holy Spirit may our prayer be...

"From ease and plenty save us;
from pride of place absolve;
purge us of low desire;
lift us to high resolve;

take us, and make us holy;
teach us your will and way.
Speak, and behold! we answer;
command, and we obey!"[152]

APPENDIX:
RESOURCES

It is impossible for us to supply all the information some will need to be able to make an informed decision about their denominational affiliation, but we share these resources to serve as a starting place for those who wish to become more informed.

Websites

www.wesleyancovenant.org

This website is filled with resources and archived informational material for those who wish to read sources from the Wesleyan Covenant Association. There are several outstanding articles and video presentations.

www.globalmethodist.org

This website is filled with resources and informational material for those who wish to read about the formation and operation of the Global Methodist Church. Of particular interest will be the online version of the Transitional Book of Doctrines and Discipline of the Global Methodist Church and other up-to-date information and possibly the FAQ section that contains step-by-step guidance for clergy and congregations who wish to join the Global Methodist Church.

www.peopleneedjesus.net

This is the website of prolific blogger, Chris Ritter, who is a member of the Global Council of the Wesleyan Covenant Association. He has a link on the front page of his website that contains a compendium of every article, blog post, or news article that he's ever read or seen about the dysfunction of The United Methodist Church and potential schism in the denomination.

www.seedbed.com

This is the website of a leading publisher for the new Methodist Movement. It is associated with Asbury Theological Seminary and provides solid resources for lay and clergy leaders. It has a combination of print, video, and web-based resources. Its "Seven Minutes Seminar" (video), Daily Text (email devotional), and New Room Conference are very helpful resources for those who are looking.

www.hackingchristianity.net

This is the website of prolific blogger, Jeremy Smith, who for many is the representative voice of the progressive movement within The United Methodist Church. We do not agree with much of what Rev. Smith writes but share it here so the reader can read and be exposed to the extremes for themselves.

Books

A Firm Foundation, **published by Seedbed**

This book was written in the early days of the Wesleyan Covenant Association to give an easily accessible rationale for the reasons the launching of a new Methodist expression was necessary. It also comes with a video companion and is well suited for small groups and church boards to use to help in decision-making.

The Next Methodism: Theological, Social and Missional Foundations for Global Methodism, **published by Seedbed and edited by Kenneth J. Collins and Ryan N. Danker**

This work is a compilation of chapters produced by some of the best and brightest thinkers of the new movement. It gives a compelling and theologically rooted foundation for the movement.

The Rise of Theological Liberalism and the Decline of American Methodism, **by James V Heidinger II and published by Seedbed**

This compendium analysis of the systematic takeover of Christian higher education by liberal and eventually progressive ideologies and its consequential impact on the American Church is a must-read for anyone who wants to know how we got to the place of such deep and systemic theological disconnect.

ENDNOTES

Introduction

1. Tolkien, J.R.R. (1991). Book 1, Chapter 2. In *The Lord of the Rings—The Fellowship of the Ring*. Harper Collins.
2. Esther 4:1 (NRSV)
3. Sinek, Simon. (2019). *Start with Why*. London: Portfolio Penguin.
4. Luke 19:7(NIV)
5. See John 13:37-38
6. Luke 19:8(NIV)
7. Luke 19:9-10 (NIV)
8. Davies, Rupert E. (editor). (1989). Wesley, John. "Thoughts upon Methodism," *Works of John Wesley*, vol. 9, The Methodist Societies: History, Nature, and Design (p. 527). Nashville, TN: Abingdon.
9. Esther 4:14 (NRSV)

Chapter 1

10. Luck, K. (April 4, 2014), Sexual Atheism: Christian Dating Data Reveals a Deeper Spiritual Malaise. *Charisma Magazine*.
11. Genesis 1:27 (NIV)
12. Genesis 2:24 (NIV)
13. Janoscik, Daniel. (Spring 2012), The Fate of Culture in J.D. Unwin's 'Sex and Culture,' *Christian Apologetics Journal*, 10(1).
14. Ephesians 3:16-19 (NIV)
15. James 2:10 (NIV)
16. James 3:1 (NIV)
17. Hebrews 13:4 (NIV)
18. 2 Corinthians 5:17 (NIV)
19. See Chapter 4. The Lord of History

Chapter 2

20. Jude 3 (NSRVue), New Standard Revised Version updated edition: retrieved from www.biblegateway.com.

21. Romans 1:26 (ESV).

22 *The Book of Discipline of the United Methodist Church,* 2016, ¶2702.1.b, p.788

https://www.cokesbury.com/book-of-discipline-book-of-resolutions-free-versions.

23. McGrath, Alister (2009). *Heresy: A History of Defending the Truth* (p. 31). Harper Collins: New York, New York.

24. Jude 2-4 (CEB).

25. *The Book of Discipline of the United Methodist Church, 2016,* Section III. Restrictive Rules, ¶17, Article I, p.31: https://www.cokesbury.com/book-of-discipline-book-of-resolutions-free-versions.

26. Philippians 2:10-11 (CEB).

27. CST Claremont School of Theology. 2022. *About CST - CST Claremont School of Theology.* [online] Available at: <https://cst.edu/about> [Accessed 3 August 2022].

28. Iliff.edu. 2022. *Purpose and Vision Statement | Iliff School of Theology.* [online] Available at: <https://www.iliff.edu/vision2022/> [Accessed 3 August 2022].

29. MTSO. 2022. *Our Mission | MTSO.* [online] Available at: <https://www.mtso.edu/about-mtso/our-aspiration/> [Accessed 3 August 2022].

30. John 1:14 (NRSV)

31. 1 Corinthians 15:14 (NRSV)

32. Bird, M. and Wright, N. T. (2019). *The New Testament in Its World* (p.750). Grand Rapids, Michigan.

33. Neuhaus, Richard John, March 2009. "The Unhappy Fate of Optional Orthodoxy: Neuhaus's Law." *First Things.* Retrieved from: *https://www.firstthings.com/article/2009/03/the-unhappy-fate-of-optional-orthodoxy* .

34 Neuhaus, Richard John, March 2009. "The Unhappy Fate of Optional Orthodoxy: Neuhaus's Law." *First Things.* Retrieved from: *https://www.firstthings.com/article/2009/03/the-unhappy-fate-of-optional-orthodoxy* .

35 & 36. Creasy Dean, K., 2010. *Almost Christian: What the Faith of Our Teenagers is Telling the American Church (p. 36).* Oxford University Press: Oxford.

37 & 38 Bates, Matthew. (2017). *Salvation by Allegiance Alone* (p. 15 and p. 199). Baker Academic: Grand Rapids.

39. Bird, Michael and Wright, N. T., 2019, *The New Testament in Its World* (p. 755). Grand Rapids, Michigan.

40. Jude 17 (NASB)

41 Lewis, C.S.,1945. *Christian Apologetics.* Retrieved from: *https://virtueonline.org/christian-apologetics-cs-lewis-1945. [Accessed August 3, 2022]*

42. Jude 3 (NRSVue)

43. Jude 24-25 (CEB)

Chapter 3

44. John 16:7 (NIV)
45. Acts 1:4-5 (NIV)
46. Acts 4:32 (NIV)
47. 2 Timothy 4:2-5 (NIV)
48. See Chapter 4. The Lord of History
49. Timothy 4:11 (NIV)
50. Colossians 4:10 (NIV)
51. Judges 21:25 (NIV)

Chapter 4

52. Romans 8:28 (NRSV)
53. 1 Chronicles 12:23
54. 1 Chronicles 12:32 (ESV)
55. 1 Samuel 2:30, ESV
56. Acts 15:1 NIV
57. Acts 15:10-10, CEB
58. Acts 15:19f NIV
59. John 17:20-21, NRSV
60. Marsh, J. (Winter 2015), "Was Wesley Anglican? Implications for Mission," *Great Commission Research Journal*, Volume 6, p. 203.
61. Matthew 28:16-20, NIV
62. Wesley, John. "Thoughts on Methodism," 1786
63. Church, A., 2022. *Our History - AME Church*. [online] AME Church. Retrieved from: <https://www.ame-church.com/our-church/our-history/> [Accessed 3 August 2022].
64. Eventually the 1792 Christian Church or "Connection" ended up as a part of the present-day United Church of Christ (UCC).
65. See Kevin M. Watson, *Old or New School Methodism: The Fragmentation of a Theological Tradition*. The word "Free" was "adopted because the new church (1) was anti-slavery; (2) wanted pews to be free to all regardless of status, rather than sold or rented (as was common); (3) promoted freedom of worship in the Holy Spirit, as opposed to stifling formality; (4) upheld the principle of "freedom" from secret and oath-bound societies (in particular the Masonic Lodge), so as to have full loyalty to Christ; (5) stood for "freedom" from the abuse of ecclesiastical authority (due to the bishop's action in allowing expulsion of 120 clergy and lay); and (6) desired its members experience "freedom" of transformation in sanctification via the Holy Spirit due to personal consecration and faith, rather than 'sin-management' or gradual growth following justification.
66 & 67. Outler, Albert C. (editor), Wesley, John. (1989). *"Catholic Spirit,"* *The Works of John Wesley* (Introduction: 4). Abingdon Press: Nashville.
68. Outler, Albert C. (editor), Wesley, John. (1985). *"Catholic Spirit,"* *The Works of John Wesley* (Volume 2: Sermons II, Sermon Number 39, p.92). Abingdon Press: Nashville.

69. Outler, Albert C. (editor), Wesley, John, *"Catholic Spirit"* (III:1)
70. Outler, Albert C. (editor), Wesley, John, *"Catholic Spirit"* (II:1)
71. Outler, Albert C. (editor), Wesley, John, *"Catholic Spirit"* (III:4)

Chapter 5
72. 1 Corinthians 15:1, NRSV
73, 74. 75, 76. Piper, E., (July 25, 2021), America's New Religion: Fake Christianity. *The Washington Times. Retrieved from: http://washingtontimes.com.*
77. Jude 3 (NRSVUE)
78 Attributed to Bishops Irenaeus and Athanasius
79. Outler, Albert C. (editor). (1984). Wesley's Standard Sermon #31: Upon our Lord's Sermon on the Mount Discourse 11. *The Works of John Wesley* (Vol. I, Sermons I (1-33), pp. 664-673). Nashville: Abingdon Press.
80. I Corinthians 15:3-4 (NIV)
81. John 14:6 (NIV)
82. Personal Class Notes
83. Eisenhower, D.D., Pbs.org. 2022. *God in the White House | American Experience | PBS.* [online] Available at: <http://www.pbs.org/godinamerica/god-in-the-white-house/> [Accessed 3 August 2022].
84. Matthew 7:24-27 (CEB)
85. Creasy Dean, K., 2010. *Almost Christian: What the Faith of Our Teenagers is Telling the American Church* (p. 25). Oxford University Press: Oxford.
86. I Samuel 3:1 (NIV)
87. Newbigin, Lesslie. *The Foolishness to the Greeks (p. 20).* Grand Rapids, MI: William B. Erdmans Publishing.
88. William J. Abraham. (2003). *The Logic of Renewal* (p. 26). Grand Rapids, MI: Willaim B. Erdmans Publishing. (internal citation: Leslie Newbigin, *Unfinished Agenda*, p. 249).
89. John 18:38 (NIV)
90. Abraham, William J. (1995). *Waking from Doctrinal Amnesia: The Healing of Doctrine in the United Methodist Church* (p.45). Abingdon Press.
91. Outler, Albert C. (editor), 1984. *The Works of John Wesley* (p. 34). Abingdon Press.
92. Outler, Albert C. (editor), 1984. *The Works of John Wesley (p. 321).* Abingdon Press.

Chapter 6
93. Philippians 3:20 (Moffatt)
94. Hauerwas, Stanlye. and Willimon, William H. (1989). *Resident Aliens* (p. 12). Nashville: Abingdon Press.
95 & 96. Kisker, Scott. (2008). *Mainline or Methodist? Rediscovering our Evangelistic Mission.* Nashville: Discipleship Resources.
97. *The Book of Discipline of the United Methodist Church 2016,* ¶105, p. 83. Retrieved from: https://globalmethodist.org/what-we-believe/
98. Matthew 7:24-27 (NRSV)

99. Abraham, William J. and Watson, David F. (2013). *Key United Methodist Beliefs* Abingdon Press.

100. Outler, Albert C. (1975). *Theology in the Wesleyan Spirit* (p. 71). Nashville: Discipleship Resources.

101. Outler Albert C. (1975). *Theology in the Wesleyan Spirit* (p. 69). Nashville: Discipleship Resources.

102 & 103 Outler, Albert C. (editor). (1984). *The Works of John Wesley* Vol. 1, Sermons I (1-33) (pp. 120-121). Nashville: Abingdon Press.

104. Watson, Kevin (April 21, 2020). What did Wesley mean by "Salvation by Faith"?. Blog Article. Retrieved from http://kevinwatson.com.

105. Warner, Laceye, (2008). "Spreading Scriptural Holiness: Theology and Practices of Early Methodism for the Contemporary Church," *The Asbury Journal*: Vol. 63: No. 1, p. 115-138. Retrieved from: *https://place. asburyseminary.edu/asburyjournal/vol63/iss1/7/*

106. Philemon 6 (NSRV)

107. *Stetzer, Ed. (Feb 2015). Evangelism Never Changes, But Methodists Do, Blog Article.*

Retrieved from http://churchleaders.com

108. *16 William Temple Quotes | ChristianQuotes.info*

109. Dylan, Bob. (1979). Gotta Serve Somebody. On *Slow Train Coming* (CD). Sony.

110. Ironically, many progressive Christians who hold to a vague notion of universal salvation want to exclude from salvation and/or heaven certain people they deem unworthy.

111. 1 Corinthians 2:1-2(NRSV)

112. Matthew 28:19-20a (NRSV)

113. Niles, Daniel T., 2012. *That They May Have Life* (p. 96). Whitefish, Montana: Literary Licensing.

114. Acts 2:41(NRSV)

115. Acts 2:47(NRSV)

116. Wikipedia. 2022. "*Tham Luang cave rescue*"[online] Available at: <https:// en.wikipedia.org/wiki/Tham_Luang_cave_rescue> [Accessed 3 August 2022].

117. Luke 10:25-37; Matthew 22:36-40

118. Warren, Rick. (2010). *The Purpose Driven Church: Growth without Compromising your Mission. Zondervan.*

119. Rev. Mike Ramsdell, Executive Director for Evangelism, Missions and Church Growth of the Central Texas Conference of the United Methodist Church, April 2020

120. Heitzrater, R.P. (1995). *Wesley and the People Called Methodist*s (p. 125). Nashville: Abingdon Press.

121. There is a need for many Christian traditionalists to read or re-read Reinhold Niebuhr's *Moral Man and Immoral Society*.

Chapter 7

122. *https://www.brainyquote.com/quotes/william_inge_149275*

123. I note again that this will not be easy but will be necessary if the Next Methodism is to be a faithful and fruitful expression of the way of Christ.

124. Dreher, Rod. (2020). *Live Not By Lies* (p. 169). New York: Sentinel.

125. Kreider, Alan. (2016). *The Patient Ferment of the Early Church* (p. 13). Grand Rapids, Michigan: Baker Academic.

126. Metaxas, Eric (2007). *Amazing Grace: William Wilberforce and the Heroic Campaign to End Slavery* (p. 278). New York: Harper Collins Publisher.

127. Hebrews 10:31

128. Dillard, Annie (1982). *Teaching a Stone to Talk: Expeditions and Encounters* (pp. 40-41). New York: Harper & Row.

129. The addition of "for the transformation of the world" in the mission statement of the United Methodist Church is redundant. True disciples of Christ transform the world by their very existence.

130. A disciple is understood as a disciplined committed follower of Christ anchored on the great commission of Matthew 28:18-20; recovery of doctrine and discipline linked to orthopraxy

131. Dillard, Annie, 1982. *Teaching a Stone to Talk: Expeditions and Encounters* (pp. 40-41). New York: Harper & Row.

132. Scazzero, Peter. (2003). *The Emotionally Healthy Church* (p. 180). Grand Rapids, Michigan: Zondervan.

133. Mark 8:35 (NRSV)

Chapter 8

134. Matthew 16:24-25 (NASB)

135. 1 Timothy 3:1 (NIV)

136. Transitional Book of Doctrines and Discipline of the Global Methodist Church Paragraph 349.4, 5. Retrieved from: https://globalmethodist.org/what-we-believe/

137. 1 Corinthians 1:23 (NIV)

138. 1 Corinthians 1:18 (CEB)

Chapter 9

139. John 16:7 (NLT)

140. Acts 4:32 (NLT)

141, 2 Corinthians 4:1 (NIV)

142. 2 Corinthians 4:2 (NIV)

143. 2 Corinthians 4:3-4(NIV)

144. 2 Corinthians 4:5 (NIV)

145. 2 Corinthians 4:6-7 (NIV)

146. 2 Corinthians 4:7 (NIV)

147. 2 Corinthians 4:8-9 (NIV)

An Invitation

148. 1 Corinthians 12:27 (ESV)

149. Philippians 3:7-8 (NRSV)

150. Philippians 3:14 (NRSV)

151. Isaiah 40:31 (KJV)

152. Verse 4, "The Voice of God is Calling," No. 436, *The United Methodist Hymnal*

ABOUT THE AUTHORS

Jeffrey E. Greenway

Jeff was raised in a Christian home, commit-
ting his life to Christ during his early teens.
It was during these formative years that God
placed a call upon his life to enter full-time
Christian service. He is a graduate of Mount
Union College (BA: Business), Asbury Theological Seminary (MDiv), and Wesley Theo-
logical Seminary (DMin: Evangelism).

Prior to becoming the Lead Pastor of the Reynoldsburg United Methodist Church near Columbus, OH, he served as President
of Asbury Theological Seminary, Superintendent of the Pittsburgh
East District of the Western Pennsylvania Conference, and as Pastor of congregations in Butler and Erie, PA. He also has extensive
denominational experience having been appointed to serve on various denominational boards and being elected by his peers to attend
and provide leadership in his denomination's highest governing
bodies. He is widely seen as a leader of leaders by his peers.

Jeff's approach to ministry is one of team building. He believes in the New Testament concept of the church being the Body
of Christ, and that every member of the Body has a distinctive role
and function in ministry. In the local church, his leadership has
been committed to helping everyone become a believer in Jesus
and finding his/her distinctive passion, gifts, and style so that they
will serve where God has intended for them to serve. Jeff is never

more excited than when new people come to a faith relationship with Jesus Christ, and then discover and use their distinct gifts and graces in the ministry of the Body.

Jeff is also passionate about Biblical preaching and discipleship. He will take a particular passage of scripture and not only help the listener understand what it means but also how to apply its truth to their personal lives. Jeff is committed to leading the church to become all that God has intended and equipped it to be. He uses his spiritual gifts of leadership, administration, preaching, teaching, and wisdom to lay out a vision for our future.

On a personal note, Jeff is married to Beth, and together they are the parents of three adult children and have eight grandchildren. He has many interests and hobbies outside of his work. He is an avid Pittsburgh Steelers, Penn State football, and Kentucky basketball fan. He also enjoys exercise, gardening, reading, traveling, and fly-fishing.

Bishop Emeritus Mike Lowry

John Michael ("Mike") Lowry was raised in a nominally Methodist home in Northern Illinois. At the beginning of his senior year in High School, the family moved to Taipei, Taiwan, where Mike graduated from Taipei American School in 1968. Returning to the United States, he enrolled at Earlham College (a Quaker-related school) in Richmond, Indiana. His sojourn with a vague agnosticism was ended by a road to Damascus experience while taking a required course in Christian Beliefs. Mike began his ministry with the Society of Friends (Quakers) sharing in pastoral leadership for Rich Square Friends Meeting in the Spring of 1972. He graduated from Earlham in 1972 with B. A. in Political Science and Religion. His intention to go to law school was interrupted by a reluctant enrollment in Seminary at Perkins School of Theology where in graduated with a Masters in Theology (M. Div.) in 1976. He received his Doctor of Ministry from Austin Presbyterian Theological Seminary in 1985.

Shortly after graduating from Perkins, he married Jolynn Darland. They celebrated their 46th anniversary in 2022. They have a son Nathan & daughter-in-law Abigail and grandsons Simon and Adam; daughter Sarah & son-in-law Steven and grandchildren Grace and Sam.

Mike was elected to the episcopacy of the United Methodist Church at the South Central Jurisdictional Conference in July 2008. He served for 13 & ½ years as the Resident Bishop of the Central Texas Conference of the United Methodist Church. During his tenure Bishop Lowry has served the larger connection of The United Methodist Church on the Executive Committee of the Council of Bishops (2012-2016), Presiding Bishop for *Path One* New Church Development (Discipleship Ministries 2009-2016), and President of the South-Central Jurisdiction College of Bishops (2010-2011). He provided leadership on a variety of institutional boards, including serving as a member of the United Theological Seminary Board of Trustees, the Texas Methodist Foundation Board, the Texas Wesleyan University Board of Trustees, and the Texas Health Resources Board of Directors. Past service includes the United Methodist Publishing House Board of Directors, the Perkins School of Theology, S. M. U. Executive Board, the Board of Trustees for Southwestern University, and the Methodist Children's Home Board of Trustees, among others.

At the time of his election and consecration as bishop in July 2008, he was serving as executive director of New Church Development and Transformation in the Southwest Texas Conference in San Antonio, Texas. Prior to that, he was senior pastor at University United Methodist Church in San Antonio, which grew from 4,800 to 5,700 members during his tenure. His previous appointments include United Methodist Churches in Austin, Corpus Christi, Harlingen and Kerrville and, while a student, serving Plymouth Park in Irving, Texas.

Prior to his election, Mike Lowry held numerous offices, including Chair of the Board of Ordained Ministry, Chair of the Board of Global Ministries' Committee on Church Extension, and Chair of the Council on Church Revitalization and Church Extension. While serving as the Executive Director for New Church

Development and Transformation in the Southwest Texas Conference, he led a successful conference capital campaign to fund new church starts.

Bishop Lowry was awarded the B'nai B'rith Award in Social Ethics by Perkins School of Theology (1976) and the Harry Denman Evangelism Award from the Central Texas Conference-Foundation for Evangelism (2015).

Upon retirement on January 1, 2022, Bishop Lowry became the Bishop in Residence at United Theological Seminary where he currently serves. He and his wife Jolynn moved to the Eastern panhandle of West Virginia to be near family.

Mike Lowry joined the Global Methodist Church at its inception as Bishop Emeritus. He now serves on the Transitional Leadership Council of the Global Methodist Church. He has a passion for Christ and for the transformation of the church as a mission post of the advancing Kingdom of God. He often encourages people to greater faithfulness to Jesus Christ by reminding them (and himself) in the midst of trials to "breathe deep, Jesus is still Lord! And that is a very good thing!"

Made in the USA
Middletown, DE
15 September 2022